LANGUAGE LiNE! FOUNDATION

John Seely

HEINEMANN
EDUCATIONAL

Contents

National Curriculum Levels and Strands

Speaking & Listening	Reading	Writing	Presentation
		5e	
		5e	
5e			
5e			
	6e		
	6e		
	6e		
	6e		
	6e		
	5d		
	5d		
	5d		
	5d		
		6e	
			Spelling 3b
	7e		
	7e		
	7e		
		6e	
		6e	
		6e	
5e			
5e			
5e			
6d			
6d			
5e, 6d			
5e, 6d			
		5b, 5e	
		5b, 5e	
		5b, 5e	
		5e	
		5b, 5e	
		6b	
7d			
	5e		
	5e		
	5e		
			Spelling 4a
	5e		
	5e		

INTRODUCTION

About this book

Language Live ! foundation is the first of three books focusing on knowledge about language for the National Curriculum. It is designed to introduce concepts about language and provide a range of materials for further study.

Language Live! is based on the belief that the study of language should not be an arid matter of artificial exercises divorced from the real language used by real people. It can and should be interesting, entertaining and directed towards real issues. The materials chosen for the foundation book draw directly from the language of everyday life and from the literature that teachers use as the centre of their work with classes of eleven and twelve year olds. In this way work on language awareness can take its proper place within an integrated approach to English.

The National Curriculum lays considerable emphasis on spoken English, both as an integral part of work in the classroom and as an important subject for study and analysis. The audiocassette accompanying the book provides a range of material on the contrasts between written and spoken English, accent and dialect, and appropriateness of language according to purpose, topic and audience. The cassette is an essential part of the way in which *Language Live!* helps students to focus on the particular qualities of spoken language.

Language Live! foundation concentrates on levels 5 and 6, while providing reinforcement and revision of relevant strands at level 4. *Language Live!* key stage three focuses on levels 6 and 7 with some coverage of levels 5 and 8, while the key stage four book will concentrate on levels 7 and 8 but provide opportunities for extension up to level 10 and considerable reinforcement at levels 5 and 6.

How to use this book

Two reference tools are provided for flexible lesson planning. The first is the matrix at the front of the book which shows the coverage of profile components and statements of attainment in individual units. The second is the 'useful words' section at the back which provides a quick reminder of the meaning of basic language terms and also shows where to find them taught in context in the book.

Cassette

Where use of the cassette is required by the text, you will see this symbol.

Most of the material on cassette is transcribed in the students' book so that classes can support their listening by reference to the text.

Cassette contents

Chapter 1 What's language for?
It's not so much fun to grunt
A funny squanny
Choice, wicked and exxy

Chapter 3 Speaking and writing
Water sounds
Waking from a nap on the beach
Willow in the wind
The storm
Another day
A Midsummers Night's onomatopoeia
Night mail
Writing speech down
Broken collar bone
Cookery corner

Chapter 4 Different Voices
Proverbs
The twa corbies
The collier's wife
Accent
Dialect 2
Wee beasties
Narrow escape
Launching the lifeboat

Chapter 5 The Right Word in the Right Place
Local radio trainee reporter

1 What's language for ?

Have you ever tried to imagine what it would be like if there were no language at all ? Not just that people couldn't talk, but that there were no such things as words, no such things as sentences...

This ↘

would become ↘
this

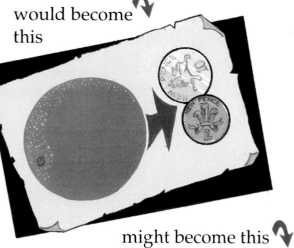

This ↘

Once upon a time there was a boy called Jack. He lived with his mother in a cottage in the country.

Jack's father was dead and Jack and his mother were very poor . . .

might become this ↘

but what would you do with this ? ↘

28 MONDAYS TO FRIDAYS

No service Saturdays or Sundays

For additional buses between Aylesbury, Wendover and Halton Camp — see Routes 55, 56, 57

For main service between Aylesbury and Tring — see Route 61

BUS ENQUIRIES ☎ AYLESBURY 84919

LIFE WITHOUT LANGUAGE

1 Think of all the things you have done today since you got up.

2 Think about the ways in which you have used language.

3 Make a list of all the things you wouldn't have been able to do if you hadn't had any language.

4 Think about other ways in which language is important in your life. Add to your list other things that you wouldn't be able to do if you had no language.

Managing without language

Sometimes we have to manage without language...

What would you do if you were the girl (and there was no one else to ask)?

WORK IT OUT
How would you communicate in each of these situations?

What to do

For each set of pictures work out what each person is trying to communicate.

Acting

1 Decide who will act each of the people.

2 Think about how you are going to get your message across.

3 Try to have the conversation without using any words at all.

Talking

Now discuss how it went.

1 What were the easiest things to communicate ?

2 What were the most difficult things ?

3 Why was this ?

It's not so much *fun* to grunt

We asked a number of people what they thought life would be like without language. These are some of the things they said.

A

A Vietnamese refugee - who was an artist - said to me, 'People just raise their voice and speak louder. And they think I'm stupid because I don't understand.' And I feel very sorry for foreigners who come here, because I identify with their problems in a society which thinks that if you can't find the words you don't have the ideas.

I remember living in Germany as a student, not knowing very much German. I found it was very difficult to be heard because of not having the words - that I had lost part of my identity. I couldn't make jokes. I had lost my sense of humour because I had no language through which to express it.

B

I mean a lot of the jokes that you make are just jokes with words. If you didn't have language it'd be a lot more difficult to amuse and entertain because you can make people laugh. I mean like Craig can just make us laugh by just saying,'Oh yeah 'n' that' and 'Ooops for the lads!' and just stupid things like that. And if you didn't have a language life would be pretty dull.

C

Well we'd be down to grimaces, gestures, body language - things like that. In a way it may well be just as full.

D

I think a world without language would actually be impossible anyway. I mean: OK, hypothetically it would be very boring but language actually just would evolve.

E

I think if language wasn't invented, it would be. Language is wonderful - what we can do with it ! We can turn it on its head, like poetry. It's just - I don't know - like a magic wheel of words pouring out. It's brilliant to have so many words that you can play with. It's not so much fun to grunt.

Thinking in more detail

1 Imagine that you suddenly found yourself in a country where no one else spoke your language. How would you feel? What would you miss most?

2 Speaker B says, 'If you didn't have a language life would be pretty dull.' Why does she say that ?

3 Do you agree with her ?

4 What do you think Speaker C means by 'grimaces, gestures, body language' ?

5 Think about what you did when you were working on page 7. What would the main problems be if we had to communicate like that all the time ?

6 Look at what Speaker D says. When you were communicating without words how did you feel ? (Did you cheat ?)

7 When people started to use language what do you think they might have found words for first ?

8 At first language was only spoken; there was no writing. What would be the problems about not having writing ?

9 What does Speaker E like so much about language ?

Language purposes

By now you should have some good ideas about what you use language for in your life. These are some of the purposes for which people use language.

A AND THE FAMILY ARE ALL WELL, ARE THEY?

B SCRABBLE

C Plant eaters

This great plant eater, *Brontotherium*, lived between 38 and 26 million years ago. It grew to about 4.5 m (15 ft) long. It had a huge double horn on its nose, and legs as thick as tree trunks.

In prehistoric times there were many plant-eating mammals, just as there are today. Their teeth were specially suited for eating plants. Some could chew soft plants. They died out when the tough grasses began to grow instead.

This curious-looking mammal, *Glyptodon*, lived in South America. It was nearly 3 m (10 ft) long. A bony shell covered its head, body and tail. This protected it like a suit of armour.

16

D Domesday book

E Filter Care

The wet and dry vacuum cleaner is designed to pick up debris and waste other household vacuums cannot. Consequently extra care must be given to the filter which, if properly maintained, will extend vacuum performance and motor life.

The machine top should be put in place ensuring that it is positioned correctly on the tank, and the three latches securely snapped shut.

Dirty filters impair suction — it will be necessary to either clean or replace following these steps

1 Unplug machine and unclip the lid
2 Remove the filter and brush grooves clean with a soft brush. It may be necessary to clean under running water. If so, let it dry naturally prior to replacement

Important
Always ensure filter is fitted flush against the underside of the lid. Failure to do so may result in motor damage thus invalidating the warranty.
USE ONLY GOBLIN-AQUAVAC BRAND REPLACEMENT CARTRIDGE FILTERS (Ref. 903-04) from Goblin Ltd or from your local Goblin Service Agent — see enclosed leaflet for details.

Wet Pick-up
To avoid the accumulation of sludge clean the filter and empty the tank before picking up liquids. Wash the accessories after use especially after picking up sticky liquids.
WARNING! DO NOT USE THE MACHINE TO PICK UP INFLAMMABLE OR CORROSIVE LIQUIDS.

Emptying
Unplug the machine from the power source and unclip the tank latches.
For liquid wastes, take the unit to a drain, remove the top and empty. WIPE THE TANK CLEAN WITH A DAMP CLOTH
For solid wastes empty the tank into a suitable receptacle

F **!!@$**¿!!!

G FIRST DIVISION

Charlton 10,513 .... (0) 0
Aston Villa Mountfield 4 .... (1) 2
McLaughlin 57 (og)
Coventry Speedie 84 .... (0) 1
Crystal Palace 10,858 .... (0) 0
Liverpool Barnes 32 Nicol 76 .... (1) 2
Luton Black 72 Nogan 74 35,312 2
Man Utd Pallister 47 38,985 .... (0) 1
Derby Co Wright 23 Pickering 75 2
Nottm Forest Clough 25 Laws 60 Hodge 67 .... (1) 3
Millwall Sheringham 79 18,065 .... (0) 1
QPR Falco 49 Clarke 83 .... (0) 2
Norwich Gordon 70 11,439 .... (0) 1
Southampton Osman 14, 74 .... (1) 2
Everton Whiteside 44, 46 19,381 .... (1) 2
Tottenham Howells 44 .... (1) 1
Man City Hendry 80 26,384 .... (0) 1
Wimbledon Bennett 88 .... (0) 1
Arsenal 13,739 .... (0) 0

OVENDEN PAPERS COMBINATION.— Luton 3, Wimbledon 4; West Ham 3, Charlton 1.

	P	W	D	L	F	A		W	D	L	F	A	Pts
Liverpool	23	6	4	1	21	7		5	4	2	18	13	**43**
Aston Villa	22	8	2	1	25	11		4	3	4	14	9	**41**
Arsenal	22	6	3	2	18	10		4	4	3	13	13	**37**
South'mpton	22	4	6	1	24	16		4	3	4	17	20	**33**
Nottm F	22	6	5	1	18	11		3	1	6	17	20	**33**
Tottenham	22	7	4	1	17	11		3	1	6	17	22	**35**
Derby C	22	5	5	2	14	10		4	2	4	12	12	**34**
Everton	22	7	4	0	25	13		2	1	8	13	20	**32**
Norwich	22	5	4	2	19	10		3	4	4	11	14	**32**
Chelsea	22	4	4	3	21	16		4	4	3	18	17	**32**
Coventry	22	4	4	4	17	18		3	6	1	11	10	**31**
Wimbledon	22	4	3	4	15	15		4	4	3	14	13	**31**
QPR	22	5	3	2	11	6		4	1	7	15	24	**31**
Man U	22	4	5	3	18	11		3	3	4	13	14	**29**
Sheff Wed	22	6	2	3	21	15		1	4	6	11	19	**27**
Man City	22	4	4	4	18	19		3	2	5	12	16	**27**
Millwall	22	3	3	4	16	12		3	5	4	8	13	**26**
Luton	22	4	2	4	14	11		3	2	7	9	17	**25**
Charlton	22	3	3	5	14	17		3	2	6	11	18	**23**
Crystal Pal	22	4	0	7	18	23		3	2	6	11	22	**23**
Everton													**22**

SOUTH EAST COUNTIES.— Div 1: Charlton 4, Chelsea 0; Arsenal 1: Fulham 1; Portsmouth 0; Cambridge 2; Leyton Orient 2, Millwall 1; Gillingham 0, Norwich 1; Tottenham 3, QPR 2; Watford 3, West Ham 1. Div 2: Aldershot 1, Southampton 0; Brighton 1, Crystal Palace 1; Brentford 2, Reading 1; Bournemouth 2, Colchester 1; Bristol C 0, Bristol R 0; Luton 4, Tottenham 2; Northampton 0, Wimbledon 0; Swindon 0, Oxford 5.

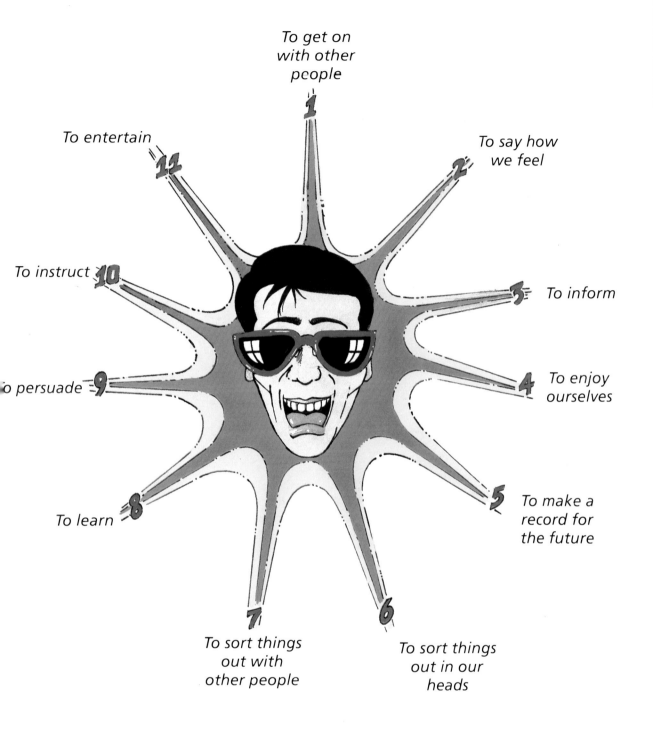

What do you think ?

1 Which of these purposes are illustrated in the picture on the opposite page ? Write down the numbers of the purposes. Against each one write the letter of the picture that goes with it.

2 What about the other purposes ? You should have four numbers without letters against them. Make up an example for each of these. Write it down against the number.

3 Any more ? If you can think of other purposes for which you use language, write them down at the bottom of the list. Think of an example for each one and write that down, too.

In the HIGH STREET

WHO SAYS WHAT ?

We overheard these snippets of conversation as we walked round the town. See if you can match the conversations to the places in the pictures. Then try to explain why you think you are right.

...it's a lot cheaper because it's a package...

...I've got the album...

...but it's a bit too big for me, I think...

...wait till it comes out in paperback...

...better value if you buy the whole bunch...

...call back later...

...a pot or a cup ?

THE WHOLE CONVERSATION

You guessed which words belonged in each place because you were able to imagine some of the rest of the conversation. Choose one of the snippets and make up the whole conversation, either acting it with a partner or writing it down.

PHRASE BOOK

When we visit a foreign country we may need to use a phrase book which explains how to say simple things and be understood. Suppose you were making up an English phrase book for someone of your age, who couldn't speak any English at all. Choose one of the places shown on this page. Make a list of the most important words and sentences the person would need to be able to use and understand in that place. For example:

At the supermarket

Can you tell me where to find . . .

I should like . . .

Can you tell me the price of . . .

fresh vegetables
cabbages
lettuce

13

A funny squanny

Not everybody talks the same. People from different places pronounce words in different ways; they speak with different accents. People from different areas use different words and grammar;they have different dialects. We asked a group of people about this.

F

I come from East Anglia in Suffolk and we've got a certain brogue and they used to say - if you's going out to get some blackberries - then you'd say, 'I know a funny squanny where you can get some blackberries.' A funny squanny, you see. Well that really meant a spot where there was plenty of blackberries existing, you see. Everything was 'funny', you see: funny squanny. I often get people come and I break into these here expressions at times. I sometimes say...Oh perhaps I haven't changed my clothes. I go up. I'll say, 'I'm just going upstairs to shiffen.' And they look: 'What was he...what did he say ?' 'I'm just going upstairs to change my clothes; put a new shift on, as they call it.' But you can...you use the word 'shiffen', you see.

G

If you go round the country, you'd find that they've all got these. They're not national; they're just local to the area, you know. Like in Yorkshire they say, 'Shut door...' What is it ? 'Put t' wood in t' 'ole.' That's how they say it: close the door.

H

My parents both originally come from Manchester. Some of the phrases they use are...like: 'It's up in Annie's room behind the wallpaper.' If we're asking for something and Mum has absolutely no intention of looking for it either because she thinks we should know where it is, she'll say, 'It's up in Annie's room behind the wallpaper.' And then:'Well I'll go to the foot of our stairs!' is a bit like 'Well knock me down with a feather !' - things like that.

E

We all have our own idioms. For example in Australia and New Zealand we can say, 'This side of the black stump' : 'I've never seen a person like that this side of the black stump,' which means 'I haven't seen someone like this for a long distance.' Or we can say things like, 'We're going into the wopwops,' which is the bush or a wild desolate area. Or, 'We're going bush,' instead of, 'we're going into the bush.' Or, 'We're going walkabout,' which is definitely Australian - which is taken from the aboriginal.

Talking points

1 Did you find any of the speakers difficult to understand ? What exactly caused the difficulty ?

2 The speakers mention a number of words and expressions. How many of them did you know already ?

3 Can you think of any other sayings like those mentioned by Speaker H ?

4 Speaker F comes from Suffolk and Speaker G from Yorkshire. What are the differences in the way they pronounce words ?

Translation, please

Copy and complete this table to include all the dialect words used by the speakers.

Their word(s)	The word(s) I would use
A funny squanny shiffen	

Choice, wicked and exxy

Language doesn't stand still. Old words die out or change their meaning and new words come into the language.

F

When I went to school up to fourteen years of age you learned a certain range of English, but since I - I'm 83 now - since I been through all these years, more words have come into the English language. And some of them are very complicated words, specially in the medical side. And you have a job to pronounce them. There's far more to learn now than there was when I was a youngster.

J

Well, there are all sorts of words which have come into the English language. Like, for instance, hoover: you'd always say, 'Oh, I'm going to go and do the hoovering.' You don't talking about 'going to use the vacuum cleaner' or whatever, and that's a brand name. And then there are other things like jacuzzi and sellotape.

H

There are a lot of sort of computerese words like 'on stream' and 'on line'. People say it with relation to diaries and meetings: 'I'll see if I can open a window for you - I'll get a window for you.' I think it's from on computers you can actually open windows on the screen and slot things in.

J

And then of course there are technical words like VDU, which is a visual display unit. And then word processing: something that just wasn't around when I was that much younger. And another thing that we didn't really have were videos. I mean that's something that's only just come in recently, and now everybody knows what a video is. Then there's the filofax. All the yuppies have got a filofax.

F

Or they bring in words like yuppies. Well you think to yourself, 'Well, what's a yuppy ?' And we've got to learn what yuppy means. In fact at the moment I don't know what the word yuppy...but I know they use it. 'You're a yuppy.' And I think, 'Well, that's not English. That's a slang word been brought in.' And these sort of things - you know - confuse you. You think to yourself, 'Well, they made that word up,' you see.

K

I just find that's really funny, that. It really goes with these trends in words, you know, of what are the sort of fashionable words to use at the time to describe things. That even varies like from school to school. Everyone here at the moment, like Craig says, are saying, 'Ooh yeah 'n' that.' And things like 'nightmare' and 'dream'. Whereas people I know from other schools say 'excellent' and 'exxy'. They even shorten 'excellent'; like everything's 'exxy exxy.'

E

Where I come from it's OK to say something's 'choice' to mean it's really wonderful. Whereas you wouldn't usually think that could possibly make sense, but it's suddenly become commonplace - and everyone's using it, and accepting it, and knowing what it's supposed to mean. Or in America, where they say something's 'bad' and it's supposed to mean 'good- the complete opposite. (It) wouldn't have been understood before but it is now.

K

The example of 'bad'...I mean there's lots of words like that used in schools now, like 'wicked' to mean something is really good, whereas you might think that it meant exactly the opposite.

SORTING IT OUT
The words these speakers describe fall into a number of groups. It's probably easier to think about them separately.

FASHIONABLE WORDS
These are words which are popular for a time with a particular group of people and then die out. You probably have your own fashionable words at the moment to describe things you like or hate a lot.

What examples of these are mentioned by the speakers ?

BRAND NAMES
Some product names (like Sellotape) become part of the language. Which of these are mentioned ?

TECHNICAL TERMS
As new things are made or discovered, so new words come into the language to describe them. Some are mentioned by the speakers - which ones ? Do you know what they all mean ?

Writing

1 Make a list of all the new words mentioned by these speakers.

2 Choose four of them and write definitions of them. Explain what they mean as a dictionary would.

summary

Think back over what you have studied in this chapter. Go through the comments and questions on this page. Use them to help you sum up what you have learned. Write answers to as many of the questions as you can.

MANAGING WITHOUT LANGUAGE

It is possible to manage without using words, but there are problems.

1 Remember what you did when you acted the story about the boy being late for school (page 7). What did you learn about the problems of communicating without words ?

IT'S NOT SO MUCH FUN TO GRUNT

You listened to some people talking about life without language.

2 What new ideas did they suggest about language ?

3 How did this change your thoughts about language ?

LANGUAGE PURPOSES

You thought about the different purposes for which we use language in our daily lives.

4 Had you ever thought about this before ?

5 What was the most interesting, or amusing, or unusual purpose that you discovered ?

6 In what ways did this work add to your understanding of language ?

IN THE HIGH STREET

7 In what ways did these two pages increase your understanding of language purposes ?

A FUNNY SQUANNY

On these pages you began to find out about accent and dialect. You will find out more about them later.

8 What do you think the word 'accent' means ?

9 What do you think the word 'dialect' means ?

10 What was the most interesting thing you learned on these pages ?

CHOICE, WICKED AND EXXY

These pages are about new words coming into English. You will learn more about this later.

11 What different kinds of new words did you learn about ?

12 What was the most interesting thing you learned on these pages ?

2 LOOKING AT WORDS

What's the best word for this ?

Which of the words in the list is the best to use when talking about it ?

lorry	container lorry	roadliner
van	tanker	transporter
articulated lorry	truck	low loader

ANOTHER WORD

You may have thought of another word which isn't on the list. The pictures and captions below give you a clue.

In Orissa a huge statue of Krishna, or Jagannath, was dragged through the streets on an enormous wheeled cart.

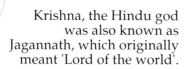

Krishna, the Hindu god was also known as Jagannath, which originally meant 'Lord of the world'.

WHERE WORDS COME FROM

This is an interesting example of one way in which language develops. If there isn't a suitable word for something then people will borrow one from another language, or will make one up. This chapter is all about words - where they come from, how they change and what they mean.

DRESSED IN BORROWED WORDS

blouse

This word was borrowed from French in the 19th century. No one quite knows how it came into English, but the modern French word blouse means 'overall, blouse, smock, or white coat'.

muslin

This also came from French ('mousseline'). They got it from the Italians ('mussolina') who used it to describe cloth made in a place they called 'Mussolo'. This was a town that the Arabs who lived there called al-Mausil.

jeans

If you thought jeans came from America you wouldn't be completely correct. The word was first used in Britain in the 16th century to describe a kind of cotton cloth. Its name goes back to the Italian city of Genoa, where it was made. Trousers were made from the cloth and they were called jeans.

denim

Denim is also imported (but, again, not from America.) It dates from the 17th century when England imported a heavy cloth from France. It was called 'serge de Nimes', because Nimes was where it was made. De Nimes soon turned into denim.

pyjamas

Pyjamas come from Pakistan. The Urdu words 'pay jama' mean 'leg clothing'.

cotton

This word came into English in the 14th century from France ('coton'), but the French got it from southern Spain, where the Arabs had a material called 'koton'.

TIME LINE

Latin used by the church

OLD ENGLISH

| 400 | 600 | 800 | 1000 |

ANGLES AND SAXONS INVADE   1066 NORMAN CONQUEST

NOW YOU TRY

Use the information on this page to make up a diagram explaining to people of your own age where some of the words came from.

1 Choose five words from this page.

2 Draw a picture of someone wearing the clothes you have chosen.

3 Write labels explaining how these clothes got their names. (Use the information on the page, but explain it in your own words.)

anorak
Eskimo word for warm outer garment with a hood

beret
French beret = cap worn by Basques (SW France) 19th C.

cap
Latin caput = head -> Latin cappa -> Old English caeppe

collar
Latin collum = neck -> collare -> Old French colier -> Middle English coler

sock
Old English socc = light shoe

PVC
polyvinyl chloride: flexible plastic used for shoes and clothing

pocket
Old French pochet = small bag attached to a piece of clothing -> 15th C poket (In some parts of Britain the word poke still means a bag.)

trainer
from train. Latin trahere = draw out -> Old French trahiner/trainer -> 15th C meaning to draw, pull -> 16th C to instruct / discipline -> to prepare for an athletic or other event -> the shoes you wear for that purpose

vest
Latin vestis = clothing -> French veste -> 17th C English meaning of sleeveless garment (like modern waistcoat) worn under a coat -> 19th C sleeveless garment worn under a shirt. (In America it means waistcoat.)

wellies
Short for wellington boots, named after 19thC Duke of Wellington

Norman French used by monarch and court

MIDDLE ENGLISH		MODERN ENGLISH		
200	1400	1600	1800	2000

People are continually finding, inventing, and borrowing new words. Sometimes they do this because they have something new they want to describe:

new WORDS

I think we'll have to call it a hyper-infra-super-micro-computer.

Sometimes words come in and out of fashion:

I think it's absolutely
fantastic,
fab,
gear,
mod,
super,
crucial,
wicked,
brill...

Yes, it is quite nice.

All the words on the opposite page have come into English since 1986

What and Why ?

You will probably know some of these words. Others may be new to you. Round the outside of the page there are:

a) pictures illustrating the meanings of some of the words.

b) clues to the meanings of some of the words.

1 Match the pictures to the words.

2 Where possible, match the clues to the words.

For each word:

3 Say what you think it means.

4 Say how you think it was made up, or where you think it came from.

INVENT A WORD

Now it's your turn. See if you can invent a word for each of these:

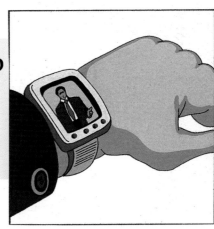

EVERY TIME I SWITCH IT ON THE SCREEN JUST SAYS HAPPY CHRISTMAS

I sometimes wonder what he's got in his head instead of brains.

water ski-ing is like ordinary ski-ing, only its on water and you get pulled along by a speedboat. Now suppose you combined the speedboat and the skis.......

Avoid the unsightly wrinkles that come with old age, use our wonder cream!

airhead **boatel** **babynap**

automaker

airmiss

wrinkly

computer virus

Near miss — an occasion when two vehicles nearly collide

bratpack

line — short for telephone line

chatline

jet-ski

To kidnap is to take someone prisoner against their will and demand a ransom.

cardswipe

YOU TOO HAVE THE CHANCE TO WIN A PRIZE OF £2000 ALL YOU HAVE TO DO...

teledish

In America cars are called automobiles, sometimes shortened to autos

A hotel is a building where you go to stay, so if you go to stay on a boat...

to bin something

def

a virus is an infection that can be passed from person to person and is not always easy to cure

brat = spoiled child or young person pack = a lot of animals that go around together

GIRLS AND GIRLS COME OUT TO PLAY

Words don't keep the same meaning forever. Some of the commonest words we use today haven't always meant what they mean now.

1250 →

A group of girls playing on the castle green

1550 ↘

A group of girls playing on the village green

1350 →

Two boys serving their masters

1650 →

Two boys chasing a dog

1250 →

A group of lads working for their master

1550 →

A group of lads on their way to school

EXPLANATION, PLEASE

Of course English has changed in many different ways since the 12th century: not just the meanings of words but how they were spoken and written down. In these examples we have used a modern spelling. The examples show how the words girl, boy, and lad have changed over the years.

Look at the pictures and the captions and then explain in your own words how each of these words has changed.

ALL CHANGE

On this page are more illustrations of common words that have changed their meanings. The examples use the words just as they were before their meanings changed. Study them carefully and then make up a short explanation, showing:

1 What the word means now.

2 What it used to mean.

3 Why you think it has changed. (This might involve some imaginative guesswork, but have a go!)

1 A polite silver cup (15th century)

2 Look at that great cloud! (9th century)

For example, if you were explaining Picture 1, you might write this:

Today 'polite' means being thoughtful towards other people in the way you speak and behave. In the middle ages, it used to mean 'polished' - as you polish silver, for example. I suppose it must have changed as people started to think that people who behaved politely were like metal that has been polished up to look its best.

3 Look at that quiz! (18th century)

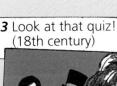

4 It was only meant as a quiz (19th century)

6 A silly woman (13th century)

5 When we travelled in Haiti we used to sleep on barbecues (17th century)

Some words developed in even more complicated ways. Use the pictures to help you explain what the word 'park' has meant at different times:

SOMEWHERE TO PARK

A lord and lady in their park (17th century)

Soldiers in the park (17th century)

king hunting in park (13th century)

A multi-storey car park (20th century)

DICTIONARY

The easiest place to discover where words came from is a dictionary. Dictionaries come in a vast range of sizes, from the Oxford English Dictionary in 20 volumes down to tiny books you can easily keep in your pocket. If you look up even a simple word in a big dictionary you will discover all sorts of very detailed information:

Origin

This tells you where the word comes from. It may include a date, a language period (like ME, which is short for Middle English, which was spoken in the late middle ages); or the foreign language (eg Fr = French) from which the word comes.

Different meanings

Many words have more than one meaning. Dictionaries usually give each meaning a number.

Pronunciation

How to say the word. Dictionaries often use special letters or symbols to show this.

> ...of the greatest number a principle of... ...political action, first enunciated by Hutcheson, 1725; shortened, later, to 'greatest h. principle', 'rule of greatest h.' **3.** How pregnant (sometimes) his Replies are? A happinesse That often Madnesse hits on SHAKS.
>
> **Happy** (hæ·pi), *a.* ME. [f. HAP *sb.*[1] + -Y[1].] †**1.** Fortuitous, chance (*rare*) −1677. **2.** Having good hap or fortune; lucky, fortunate; favoured by circumstance ME. †**b.** Blessed, beatified −1700. **3.** Characterized by or involving good fortune. (Now used only in association with senses 4 and 5.) ME. **4.** Having the feeling arising from satisfaction with one's circumstances or condition; also: Glad, pleased 1525. **5.** Apt, dexterous; felicitous ME. **6.** *colloq.* (*joc.*) Slightly drunk 1770. **1.** Any h. concourse of Atoms HALE. **2.** The h. seat of liberty 1741. **b.** If yee know these things, h. are ye if ye doe them *John* 13:17. Phr. *Of h. memory.* **3.** Many h. returns DICKENS. **4.** Better be h. then wise 1562. H. as a king GAY. **5.** He was apt and happie in armes LD. BERNERS. A most h. thought SHERIDAN, reply (*mod.*). Phr. *Happy dispatch*: see HARA-KIRI.
>
> †**Happy,** *v.* 1600. [f. prec.] To render happy −1632.
>
> **Ha·ppy-go-lu·cky.** 1672. **A.** *adv.* Just as it may happen; haphazard.

Part of speech

This is sometimes called word class. It tells you how the word is used in a sentence. The ones you will see most often in a dictionary are:

a (or adj) = adjective

ad (or adv) = adverb

n (or sb) = noun

v (or vb) = verb

Examples

For each of the meanings, there is a sentence, or part of a sentence showing how the word is used.

Questions

1 How easy would you find it to use a dictionary like this ? Why ?

2 What kinds of people would find this sort of dictionary useful and why ?

3 Most people have a good idea of what 'happy' means. So why put it in a dictionary at all ? (You should be able to think of a number of different answers to this question.)

Little DICTIONARY

Pocket dictionaries, and dictionaries written for particular kinds of reader contain less information. They often do things differently, too.

1

happy *a.* **(-ier, -iest)** contented, pleased; fortunate; pleasing. **happy-go-lucky** *a.* taking events cheerfully. **happily** *adv.*, **happiness** *n.*

2

...usually intended to startle any observers.

happy *adjective*
1. feeling or showing contentment or plea-sure: 'she is *happy* in the new job'. *Usage*: 'it was a *happy* decision to leave when we did' (= lucky).
2. (*informal*) having an excessive liking for: 'the new sheriff is *trigger-happy*'. *Word Family*: **happily**, *adverb*; **happiness**

3

happy

"**Happy** birthday to us!"

Questions

Answer these questions for each of the dictionaries illustrated.

1 Which of the kinds of information listed on the opposite page does it contain ?

2 Does it contain anything that isn't there ?

3 Who would find this kind of dictionary most useful ?

Writing

Now you have a try at making up dictionary entries.

1 Choose a word from the list below.

2 Choose one of the dictionaries shown on this page (not the opposite page !)

3 Make up a definition of the word to go in that dictionary.

4 Choose a second dictionary from this page and make up a definition for that.

book	clean	clumsy	dark
feeble	football	high	horse
leave	rush	sad	school
teacher	watch	write	

MAKING UP A DICTIONARY

You may have wondered how people go about writing a dictionary. The example on page 26 may give you a clue ▽

The dictionary-maker (or 'lexicographer') collects examples of how words are used. These are stored on cards:

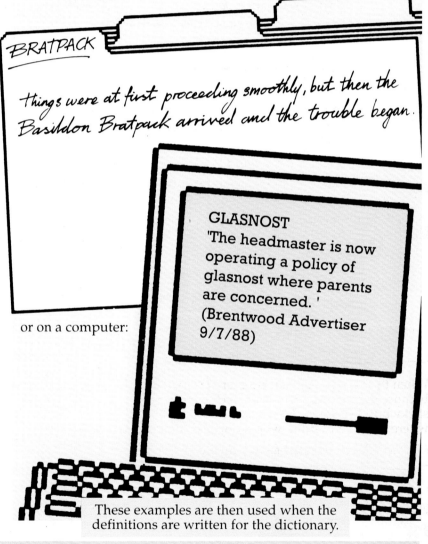

BRATPACK

things were at first proceeding smoothly, but then the Basildon Bratpack arrived and the trouble began.

or on a computer:

GLASNOST
'The headmaster is now operating a policy of glasnost where parents are concerned.'
(Brentwood Advertiser 9/7/88)

These examples are then used when the definitions are written for the dictionary.

Happiness (hæ·pinès). 1530. [f. as prec. + -NESS.] The quality or condition of being happy. **1.** Good fortune or luck; success, prosperity. **2.** The state of pleasurable content of mind, which results from success or the attainment of what is considered good 1591. **3.** Successful or felicitous aptitude, fitness, or appropriateness; felicity 1599.
1. Wish me partaker in thy happinesse, When thou do'st meet good hap SHAKS. **2.** Oh H.! our being's end and aim! Good, Pleasure, Ease, Content! whate'er thy name POPE. Phr. *Greatest h. of the greatest number:* a principle of moral and political action, first enunciated by Hutcheson, 1725; shortened, later, to 'greatest h. principle', 'rule of greatest h.' **3.** How pregnant (sometimes) his Replies are? A happinesse That often Madnesse hits on SHAKS.
Happy (hæ·pi), a. ME. [f. HAP sb.¹ + -Y¹.] †**1.** Fortuitous; chance (*rare*) –1677. **2.** Having good hap or fortune; lucky, fortunate; favoured by circumstance ME. †**b.** Blessed, beatified –1700. **3.** Characterized by or involving good fortune. (Now used only in association with senses 4 and 5.) ME. **4.** Having the feeling arising from satisfaction with one's circumstances or condition; also: Glad, pleased 1525. **5.** Apt, dexterous; felicitous ME. **6.** *colloq.* (*joc.*) Slightly drunk 1770.
1. Any h. concourse of Atoms HALE. **2.** The h. seat of liberty 1741. **b.** If yee know these things, h. are ye if ye doe them *John* 13:17. Phr. *Of h. memory.* **3.** Many h. returns DICKENS. **4.** Better be h. then wise 1562. H. as a king GAY. **5.** He was apt and happie in armes LD. BERNERS. A most h. thought SHERIDAN, reply (*mod.*). Phr. *Happy dispatch*: see HARA-KIRI.
†**Happy,** *v.* 1600. [f. prec.] To render happy –1632.
Ha·ppy-go-lu·cky. 1672. **A.** *adv.* Just as it may happen; haphazard.

Make up your own dictionary

You are writing a new dictionary. On the facing page are some of the examples that you have found to illustrate the meanings of these words:

sloom   frangly   widderbight

1 Work out from the examples what each word means.

2 Write a full dictionary definition for each one:

Part of speech	Pronunciation
Meaning	Examples

1

The day did not, however, end happily for Vera. She walked out of the house angrily and without looking where she was going. As we walked across the farmyard she slipped in some sloom and fell full length in a cattle trough !

(Adventures of a vet)

Stone and concrete that are not regularly cleaned will soon show signs of sloom. This green moss-like growth is not harmful, but it can be a nuisance and so should always be cleaned off.

(Farming Times)

The geriatric horse and groom
Clattered through the slimy sloom.

(Rhyme of the ancient farrier)

2

- So what did she say ?

- Not a lot.

- But she must have said something.

- No - she were so frangly she could scarcely say a word.

- Frangly ? I'd have thought she would have just laughed it off.

- Not her. It was the only shopping bag she had.

(Overheard in a bus queue)

When you're feeling frangly count up to ten before you speak.

(Popular saying)

During the summer months, especially on hot sultry days, when cattle are tormented by flies, they sometimes become frangly. Then they may - without warning - charge up and down the meadows tossing their heads and threatening to attack anyone who gets in their way.

(Advice for walkers on the Offa's Dyke Path)

When they got home their mother was furious because their clothes were covered with the tiny sticky burrs of the widderbight - they hadn't noticed where they were sitting when they had their picnic !

(Further adventures of the famous three by Edith Burton)

3

The fields around the town are a picture in Spring, when they are covered with a mass of pale yellow widderbight flowers.

(Basingstoke and its surroundings : a guide for tourists)

It is not generally known that there is not one Widderbight, but three. As well as the Common Widderbight, which everone knows for its tiny yellow flowers and sticky burrs, there are also Devil's Widderbight, which occurs locally in parts of Hampshire, and Stinking Widderbight, which is now confined to West Herefordshire.

(Wayside Flowers and Grasses)

A treasure-store of words

Sometimes people run short of words:

Can you think of a different word to replace nice each time it appears in this letter ? (You'll need six words altogether.)

STUCK FOR A WORD ?

Sometimes people can't think of exactly the word they want. One solution to this problem is to use a thesaurus. There are different types of thesaurus. Some are arranged by subject:

Yesterday it was a nice day, so we thought it'd be a nice idea to go out. Rachel and Diane wanted to go to the Sports Centre because they've got some really nice new tennis courts, but Dad said he wanted to go to the seaside.

So that's what we did. I took my swimming costume (you know - the nice red one) and Diane took hers, because we thought it would be nice to have a swim. We had a very nice drive down to Hastings

Others are arranged alphabetically, like dictionaries. They give lists of words that have similar meanings. These are called synonyms. (In this example **glad** and **pleased** are synonyms.)

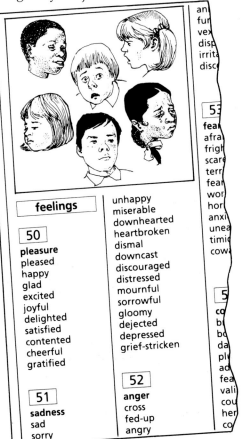

feelings	unhappy
	miserable
50	downhearted
	heartbroken
pleasure	dismal
pleased	downcast
happy	discouraged
glad	distressed
excited	mournful
joyful	sorrowful
delighted	gloomy
satisfied	dejected
contented	depressed
cheerful	grief-stricken
gratified	
	52
51	**anger**
sadness	cross
sad	fed-up
sorry	angry

misery, anguish, distress, discomfort, 2. bane, annoyance; calamity, misfortune, thorn in one's flesh, cross to bear.

happy *adj.* **1** *I'm so happy that you could visit us. My birthday was a happy occasion;* glad, pleased, delighted, content, contented, gratified; *Slang* tickled, tickled pink; gay, cheerful, in high spirits, elated, joyous, overjoyed, exhilarated, blissful, rapturous, ecstatic, exultant, gleeful, transported, rhapsodic, jubilant, flushed with pleasure, exuberant, in the seventh heaven; pleasant, pleasing, delightful, gratifying, cheering, joyful. **2** *Wasn't it a happy coincidence that I bumped into you ?*; fortunate, lucky, auspicious, favourable, felicitous, propitious; convenient, opportune, meet, timely, seasonable, fitting, fit, advantageous, agreeable.

Ant. 1 sad, unhappy, sorry, sorrowful, displeased, discontented; despondent, forlorn, miserable, gloomy, melancholy, depressed, joyous, mournful, sombre; down in the mouth, down in the dumps. **2** unfortunate, unlucky, luckless, inauspicious; unfitting, unseasonable.

harass *v.* **1** *The retreating army was harassed by the enemy:* attack repeatedly, raid frequently, assault continually, beset, besiege. **2** *If you'll stop harassing me I can finish this work:* torment, pester, badger, harry, worry, disturb, annoy, irritate, distress, bother, irk, vex, plague, hound, discommode, exasperate

COMPUTER THESAURUS

Some word processors will do a lot more than just store and print your writing. Many will check your spelling for you, and some will even help out if you are stuck for a word. But you have to be careful. A thesaurus can produce very strange results if you don't use it sensibly:

I saw three ships go sailing by.
see: behold glimpse look mind sight spot watch witness

I watched three ships go sailing by.
ship: craft cruiser freighter frigate ketch liner oceanliner sailboat schooner steamship vessel yacht

I watched three vessels go sailing by.
sail: coast drift float fly glide soar
by: adjacent around aside at atop beside near nearby on

I watched three vessels go gliding on.
vessel: bottle bucket caddy can canister flask jar pail

I watched three buckets go gliding on.
glide: coast crawl creep prowl skate skim skulk slick slide slink slither sneak steal wiggle wriggle writhe

I watched three buckets go wriggling round.

HAPPY ?

Use the words in the examples to replace **happy**, **happily** etc in this passage:

James was very happy when his grandfather gave him money for his birthday.

'I couldn't think what to get you,' said his grandfather. 'But if you're happy to buy yourself something you really want, then I shall feel very happy.'

Happily it was a Saturday, so James could go straight down to the shops. On the way he met Anna, who wished him a Happy Birthday.

LEAGUE TABLE

Choosing exactly the right word means that you need to know the 'strength' of words. It's interesting to try to put words which have a similar meaning into a league table. You put the weakest at the bottom and the strongest at the top:

furious

angry

vexed

cross

annoyed

fed up

irritated

discontented

displeased

(You may not agree with this one - but it's our version.)

Try doing the same with these lists of words:

afraid	anxious	cowardly
fearful	frightened	horrified
scared	terrified	timid
uneasy	worried	adventurous
bold	brave	cool
courageous	daring	fearless
heroic	plucky	valiant

Make a thesaurus

1 Try making your own thesaurus. Make a list of words that describe size. You will probably find it easier to start by looking for synonyms for these words:

fat   thin   tall   short

2 Take one of your lists and turn it into a league table.

Other word books

Happy, Bomb Happy. A World War II expression to describe one in a state of near hysteria induced by bombing, which often took the form of wild elation of the spirits.

Call no man happy. Properly, "Call no man happy till he dies, he is at best fortunate". It implies that no man can be called happy until his life has ended happily. The saying is attributed by Herodotus(*Histories*, I, 32) to Solon and is also used by Sophocles (*Œdipus Tyrannus*, 1192) and Aristotle.

Happy as a clam. *See* CLAM.

Happy as Larry. Very happy. An Australian expression. It is suggested that the original Larry may have been Larry Foley (1847-1917), the noted boxer.

Happy dispatch. *See* HARI-KIRI.

A happy expression. A well-turned phrase; one especially apt.

Happy Family. In travelling menageries, etc., the name given to an assortment of animals living together peaceably. The phrase is now more usually associated with the children's card game.

Happy-go-lucky. Thoughtless, indifferent, carefree.

Happy hunting ground. The North American Indian's HEAVEN. Figuratively, where one finds happy leisure occupation.

Happy is the country that has no history. The old proverb implies that such a nation avoids the wars, rebellions, etc., that forms so much of human history. Gibbon in *The Decline and Fall of the Roman Empire* (ch. iii) says:
Hisory, which is, indeed, little more than the register of the crimes, follies, and misfortunes of mankind.

Happy. The inevitable nickname of anyone surnamed Day: late C.19-20: mostly services'. (Bowen.) Ex *O, happy day!*

happy, adj. Slightly (and, properly used, cheerfully) drunk: coll.:1770(OED). Marryat.—2. As suffix in, e.g. *bomb-happy, flak-happy*, with nerves shattered by exposure to imminent death or mutilation; or, as in *demob-happy*, reckless by reason of impending escape from present circumstances:WW2 and after: orig. Services, > gen. coll. (P.B.)

Happy and Chatty, the. HM cruiser *Immortalité*: RN:when, in 1895-8, she was on the China Station under Sir Edward Chichester. (Bowen.) Partly rhyming, partly allusive to her condition.—2. Hence applied to any slack-disciplined, untidy ship: nautical: C.20.

happy as a boxing kangaroo in fog time. Thoroughly discontented: Aus. coll: C.20 (B., 1942) Cf. the variants cited by Wilkes.

happy as a pig ... See happy as pigs ...

happy as Larry, (as). Very happy; delighted at the way things have turned out: Brit. and Aus. coll.: late C.19-20. Prob. ex Northern dial.

happy as pigs in muck, (as). Very happy (though perhaps rather dirty); esp. quite content with one's surroundings; low: since ca. 1870. (Gerald Kersh, *Faces in a Dusty Picture*, 1944.) Also *happy as a pig in muck*. Cf. US *pig in clover*.

happy days. Strong ale and beer mixed: public-houses, (esp. at Glasgow); from ca. 1920.

happy days! A toast that has something of the quality of a c.p.: prob ca. 1910. It occurs in 'Bartimeus',*Naval Occasions*, 1914, with the reply *Salue!*—from either Sp. *salud!*, or, more prob., Fr. *salut!*

happy dosser. See dosser.

happy Eliza. A female salvationist; 1887—ca.1910. Ex a broadside ballad that points to 'Happy Eliza and Converted Jane' as 'hot 'uns in our time'.

happy-ender. A story with a happy end: coll. (esp. in the book-world): late C.19-20. Berta Ruck. 1935.

happy family. A collection of various animals, of different natures, living quietly in one cage: 1845-1915. Albert Smith. *Natural History of the Gent*, 1847.

happy hours. Flowers: rhyming s., mainly theatrical: late C.19-20. Franklyn, *Rhyming*.

Words often have special meanings in slang. There are special dictionaries which list and explain these.

In this country Gyles Brandreth has written many books containing 'Daffy Definitions'. These are from his 'Dizzy Dictionary'.

DIZZY DICTIONARY

climate: what you do with a ladder
code: having a running nose
coincide: flat surface of penny, etc

D

dandelion: big cat very fussy about its appearance
debate: lure for de fish
deceit: where to sit down
deign: person from Denmark
Delilah: inflatable air bed
diet: Welshman's food
dogma: puppy's mother
drawing-room: dentist's surgery

E

each: minor irritation
eagle: what all men are created
earwig: hairpiece with built-in hearing aid
e.g.:   what a h.e.n. lays
etching: what a dog with fleas does
eureka: exclamation, as in, 'Eureka garlic!'
explain: to parachute
eyebrow: very intellectual

F

faith: the part of a person you recognize
fete: garden party worse than death
fever: when one person helps another out
fiddlesticks: what you play a violin with
fjord: Norwegian car

123

Things to do

1 Make up a conversation that uses some of the expressions listed in the *Slang Dictionary* or the *Dictionary of Phrase and Fable*.

2 Make up your own dictionary of all the words you can think of that people your age use when they want to express their approval and disapproval of something. Give the word, its meaning, and an example of how it might be used.

3 Make up your own crazy definitions of words. You can think of your own, or choose from these lists:

school	lesson	teacher	homework
exam	holiday	weekend	
TV	film	cinema	book
magazine	comic	newspaper	radio
record	pop	rock	disco

summary

DRESSED IN BORROWED WORDS

When speakers of a language need to describe something new, they often borrow the words they need from other languages. Often these words change after they have been borrowed and people forget where they have come from. Good examples of this can be found in the words we use for clothing and materials. Words that have been borrowed are sometimes called loan words.

NEW WORDS

People also make up new words to describe new things. They sometimes do this by joining together words that already exist - or combining parts of words. Every year many new words come into the language in this way. Some soon go out of fashion, but others last and become part of the language. Words that have been invented like this are sometimes called coinings.

GIRLS AND GIRLS COME OUT TO PLAY

Words don't keep the same meaning forever. As time passes, they change their meanings. Often there is only a slight difference, but sometimes a word changes almost out of recognition. Just as new words can come into the language, so old words pass out of use and 'die'.

BIG DICTIONARY...LITTLE DICTIONARY

A dictionary provides a lot of information about a word: where it came from, how to pronounce it, what it means, which word class it belongs to, and how it is used. The bigger the dictionary, the more of this information it provides.

MAKING UP A DICTIONARY

Dictionaries are based on examples of how words are used. The lexicographer (dictionary-maker) studies these examples and then uses them to write definitions and give other information about the word.

A TREASURE-STORE OF WORDS

Another useful word-book is the thesaurus. This lists words alphabetically, or by theme. It provides lists of words with similar meanings (or synonyms).

OTHER WORD BOOKS

Other word reference books include dictionaries of popular sayings and dictionaries of slang. People also make up humorous word-books.

WHICH CAME FIRST ?

Many people think that writing is 'better' and more important than speaking. As a result they criticise the way people speak because it is different from 'correct' written English. They also expect speakers to pronounce all the letters in a word - as if English started as a written language and then we all learned to pronounce it.

In fact all languages started as speech. Then they were written down. So writing is a way of putting language down on paper and not the other way round: All the letters that are used to spell English words are only a method of putting the sounds of those words down on paper.

WRITING IT DOWN

Different languages use different systems for turning speech into writing. Some, like Chinese, write down whole words.

This may seem strange but you also use a similar system in school. All these symbols work in a similar way to Chinese writing:

Armenian	*ել Հրամում էիր, և դա կրծքին տակ* *Ս.նյում էր Հայարո, անշութ ս.մզին*
Balinese	ᬒᬧᬳᬶᬲ᭄ᬳᬬᬦᬳᬸᬭᬳᬡᬢᬸᬮᬶ᭄ᬳᬦᬧᬓᬳᬶᬫᬶᬲ᭄ᬳᬢᬦᬳᬕᬳ᭄᭞ ᬓ᭄ᬭᬢᬦ᭄ᬮᬸᬲᬶᬦᬢ᭄ᬳᬸᬧᬲᬳᬶᬳᬶᬗᬶᬭᬤᬯᬸᬬᬹᬕ᭄ᬳᬶᬔ
Buginese	ᨕᨒ ᨆᨚᨆᨚᨊ ᨊᨘᨅᨚᨆᨚᨊ ᨆᨚᨒᨚ ᨕᨓᨚ ᨔ
Burmese	ဘုရားသခင်သည်။ သားတော်ဘ ...တိုင်း ပွတ်ဆိုလဲ တ

Other languages use an alphabet to write down the separate sounds of the language.

SPEECH AND WRITING

There are big differences in the way we use words in speech and writing. This is because of the situations in which they are used.

SEE THAT SHOP OVER THERE ? GO TO THE LEFT OF IT, ALL RIGHT ? THEN YOU'LL SEE A SORT OF BIG PAVEMENT.....

In the High street there is a branch of Boots. Just to the left of it is the start of the pedestrian precinct.

writing SOUNDS

How would you speak all the sounds in this comic strip?

Now try making up the 'sound words' to fit each of these pictures.

1

2

3

4

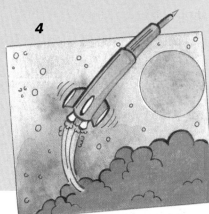

WATER SOUNDS

Sug sug buggly dug
Goes the water in the plug

Anna Chan (5)

WATER WORDS

babble	bubble	dribble	drip
drop	guggle	gurgle	gush
murmur	ooze	ripple	slosh
splash	splutter	spout	spurts
putter	squirt	surge	trill

Try your hand at making up sequences of water sounds. Invent some words of your own and use some from the list - or other real words that you can think of.

SOUNDS AND LETTERS

We divide the sounds of English into two groups, according to how we form them when we speak. Speech sounds are formed by air coming from our lungs which we make vibrate in different ways.

CONSONANTS

When we pronounce consonants we block for a moment the air passing through our mouths. To do this we use our lips, or teeth, or tongues, or other parts of the mouth and throat.

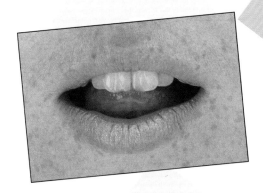

What parts of the mouth do you use to make the sounds shown in these words ?

shop   **f**eet   **m**at   **th**in   **c**ut

VOWELS

When we pronounce vowels we do not stop the air passing through our mouths. We vibrate the vocal chords in our throats and then alter that sound by shaping our mouths.

Say the vowels marked in these words. Say them in the same order. What happens to your mouth as you say them ?

h**u**t   b**a**t   g**e**t   b**i**t   p**u**t   r**oo**t

SAYING AND SPELLING

We make many different sounds when we speak English - over forty of them. When we write we only have the twenty-six letters of the alphabet to spell them all. This means that some letters have to work very hard. Look at the ways in which the letter 'e' is used in the words on this page: it makes different sounds and sometimes no sound at all.

CONSONANTS

1 Some consonants are easy. What sound do you expect when you meet each of these letters in a word ?

   d   f   j   l   m   v

2 Some consonant letters are used for more than one sound. What sounds are these letters used to spell ?

   c   g

3 Some consonant letters are regularly combined. What sound do these pairs of letters usually make ?

   ch   sh   ng

4 This pair spells two different sounds. What are they and what is the difference ?

   th

VOWELS

There are over twenty vowel sounds in English and only five vowel letters: **a,e,i,o,u**. So the rules describing how we spell the different vowel sounds are very complicated.

These two groups of words illustrate one of those rules. Can you explain what it is ?

hat	hate
bit	bite
rob	robe
tun	tune

WEATHER WORDS

*W*aking from a nap on the beach

Sounds like big
rashers of bacon frying.
I look up from where I'm lying
expecting to see stripes

red and white. My eyes drop shut,
stunned by the sun.
Now the foam is flame, the long
troughs charcoal, but

still it chuckles and it sizzles,
burns and burns, it never gets done.

The sea is that
fat.

May Swenson

*W*illow in the wind

The wind surges,
Seething through the tree,
Buffeting its branches,
So delicate to defy
This tenuous tide.
Trees tumble in full sail,
Brave mariners of the land.

John Cunliffe

*T*he storm

Without warning a snake of black cloud rises in the sky.
It hisses as it runs and spreads its hood.
The moon goes out, the mountain is dark.
Far away is heard the shout of the demon.

Up rushes the storm a moment after
Rattling an iron chain in its teeth
The mountain suddenly lifts its
Trunk to the heavens
And the lake roars like a wild beast.

Ashok B. Raha, translated by Lila Ray

Thinking about the poems

These writers have tried to describe the sounds of their subjects. For each poem:

1 Pick out the words that describe sounds.

2 Choose three sound words that you like. Explain why you think each one is a good word to use.

Writing

Choose your own weather subject and write a poem or description that includes the sound of the weather. You can use 'real' words and/or words you have made up. You may find the words in these lists helpful.

WIND WORDS		RAIN WORDS
blast	puff	bucket down
blow	rage	drip
boom	roar	drizzle
breathe	scream	drop
buzz	screech	patter
howl	sigh	pour
hum	storm	shower
moan	wail	sleet
murmur	whine	spit
mutter	whisper	sprinkle
pipe	whistle	teem

SOUND patterns

These two poems collect together a complete pattern of sounds to describe their different subjects. One uses normal words; the other uses made up words and groups of letters. They are good poems to read aloud - on your own, or even better in a group. If you work in a group you can divide them up so that different people speak different words and lines.

Another day

Boys shout,
Girls giggle,
Pencils write,
Squiggle squiggle.
Get it wrong,
Cross it out,
Bell's gone !
All out !

Balls bounce,
Hands clap,
Skipping ropes,
Slap slap.
Hand-stands,
By the wall.
Sara Williams
Best of all.
Boys fight,
Girls flee,
Teacher's gone
And spilt
His tea !
Clatter bang !
Big din !
Whistle goes,
All in !

All quiet,
No sound,
Hear Worms,
Under ground.
Chalk squeaks,
Clock creeps,
Head on desk,
Boy sleeps.

Home time !
Glory be !
Mum's got
Chips for tea.
Warm fire,
Full belly,
Sit down,
Watch telly.

Bed time,
Creep away,
Dream until,
Another day.

John Cunliffe

A Midsummer Night's onomatopoeia

tp.

tp tp.

tp tp thmp.

thmp thmp thMP THMP.

THMP THMP THUMP.

CLUNK.

Can we stop now, dad ?

We haven't gone very far, Jo.

Sure. Can I have another mint ?

You ate them all.

aw.

Can't you appreciate the country, Jo ?

It's boring. I wanna watch TV. It's too quiet.

But if you listen you can

Yeah, yeah, the sounds of nature, I've heard it all

before.

Just try it, Jo. Just listen.

aw, gimme a break, dad.

Try it.

awww...

shh.

.

.

.

bip.

bipbip.

bipbipbip.

tweeeeeep.

QUARK !

phlaphlaphlaphlaphlaphlap.

mip.

gwurk.

mip.

gwurk.

.

.

.

bzzzzzzZZZZZZZZZZzzzzzzzzZZZZt.

snapt.

rustlerustle.

bip.

QUARK !

bzzzzzmiddip.

glp.

mip.

QUARK !

zzt.

bipbip.

phlap.

.

.

.

There, y'see ? Take time to stop and listen and

Sure. Can we go home now ? I'm missing the

football game.

OK, Jo. Let's go.

THUMP THMP THMP.

THMP THmp thmp thmp.

thmp tp tp.

to.

.

.

Kieran Macdonald (13)

Now you try
Write your own sound pattern. Choose your own subject, or take one from this list:

Getting up in the morning

Train journey

Stuck on the motorway

Lost in space

The poet W.H.Auden was asked to write the sound track for a film. It was about how the night mail train takes the mail from London to Scotland. He imitated the sound of the train in the rhythm of his poem.

Night Mail

This is the night mail crossing the border,
Bringing the cheque and the postal order,
Letters for the rich, letters for the poor,
The shop at the corner and the girl next door,
Pulling up Beattock, a steady climb-
The gradient's against her but she's on time.

Past cotton grass and moorland boulder,
Shovelling white steam over her shoulder,
Snorting noisily as she passes
Silent miles of wind-bent grasses;
Birds turn their heads as she approaches,
Stare from the bushes at her blank-faced coaches;
Sheepdogs cannot turn her course,
They slumber on with paws across;
In the farm she passes no one wakes
But a jug in a bedroom gently shakes.

Dawn freshens, the climb is done.
Down towards Glasgow she descends
Towards the steam tugs, yelping down the glade
of cranes
Towards the fields of apparatus, the furnaces
Set on the dark plain like gigantic chessmen.
All Scotland waits for her;
In the dark glens, beside the pale-green sea lochs,
Men long for news.

Letters of thanks, letters from banks,
Letters of joy from the girl and the boy,
Receipted bills and invitations
To inspect new stock or visit relations,
And applications for the situations,
And timid lovers' declarations,
And gossip, gossip from all the nations,

News circumstantial, news financial,
Letters with holiday snaps to enlarge in,
Letters with faces scrawled in the margin.
Letters from uncles, cousins and aunts,
Letters to Scotland from the South of France,
Letters of condolence to Highlands and Lowlands,
Notes from overseas to the Hebrides;
Written on paper of every hue,
The pink, the violet, the white and the blue,
The chatty, the catty, the boring, adoring,
The cold and official or the heart's outpouring,
Clever, stupid, short and long,
The typed and the printed and the spelt all wrong.

Thousands are still asleep
Dreaming of terrifying monsters
Or a friendly tea beside the band at Cranston's or
Crawford's;
Asleep in working Glasgow, asleep in well-set
Edinburgh,
Asleep in granite Aberdeen.
They continue their dreams
But shall wake soon and long for letters.
And none will hear the postman's knock
Without a quickening of the heart,
For who can bear to feel himself forgotten?

W H Auden

Listening to the sound of the poem

1 Read the first two lines of the poem aloud. How do the words imitate the sound of the train ?

2 Now try reading line 3. How does the rhythm change here ? Why do you think it changes ? What might the train be doing ?

3 Read the second section of the poem (from 'Past cotton grass...' to '...gently shakes.') What sound words does it contain ? How does the rhythm of it compare with the first section ? Is there anything in the sound of the words that tells us this is an old-fashioned steam train ?

4 Now read the third section. What sound words does it contain ? How does the rhythm of it compare with the first two sections ?

Group reading

Section four (from 'Letters of thanks...' to '...the spelt all wrong.') is a good one to read aloud in a group.

1 Read it carefully on your own and think about what it says and how it ought to sound.

2 Discuss it. Think about these points:

- how can it be divided between the members of the group ?

- should any lines or words be spoken by more than one person ? - should some lines be divided up into small sections ?

- is it possible (and a good idea) to have background sound effects made by some members of the team ?

3 Plan your reading: make sure that everyone knows what they are supposed to be doing.

4 Practise your reading.

writing (SPEECH) down

When you try to write down exactly what people say, you find out just how different speech is from writing. In fact if you just write down the words they speak and nothing else it hardly looks like English at all.

So people usually change things to make it easier to read.

i come from east anglia in suffolk and weve got a certain brogue and they used to say if yous going out to erm get some blackberries

TRANSCRIPT

i come from east anglia in suffolk and weve got a certain brogue and - they used to say - if yous going out to - erm - get some blackberries then you'd say i know a funny squanny where you can get some blackb blackberries a funny squanny you see / well that really meant a - a spot where - there there was plenty of blackberries existing you see / everything was funny you see funny squanny i often get people come and I break into these here expressions at times / i sometimes say - oh perhaps I haven't changed my clothes / i go ups - ill say im just going upstairs to shiffen / and they look / what was he - what did he say / im just going upstairs to change my clothes / put a new shift on as they call it / but you can you use the word /shiffen you see

PUNCTUATED AS SPEECH

I come from East Anglia in Suffolk and we've got a certain brogue and they used to say - if you's going out to get some blackberries - then you'd say, 'I know a funny squanny where you can get some blackberries.' A funny squanny, you see. Well that really meant a spot where there was plenty of blackberries existing, you see. Everything was 'funny', you see: funny squanny. I often get people come and I break into these here expressions at times. I sometimes say...Oh perhaps I haven't changed my clothes. I go up. I'll say, 'I'm just going upstairs to shiffen.' And they look: 'What was he...what did he say ?' 'I'm just going upstairs to change my clothes; put a new shift on, as they call it.' But you can...you use the word 'shiffen', you see.

WRITTEN ENGLISH

I come from East Anglia in Suffolk and we have a certain brogue. If I was going out to get some blackberries, I would say, 'I know a funny squanny where you can get some blackberries.' A 'funny squanny' meant a spot where there were plenty of blackberries growing. Everything was 'funny'. I often have visitors and I sometimes break into such expressions. For example, perhaps I haven't changed my clothes. I'll say, 'I'm just going upstairs to shiffen.'

They look at each other and think, 'What was he...what did he say ?'

'I'm just going upstairs to change my clothes; put a new shift on, as they call it.'

Instead of that I use the word 'shiffen'.

What's the difference ?

Study all three versions carefully.

1 What are the main differences between them ?

2 Which do you think is the clearest ?

3 Which is the closest to what the man said ?

4 When might each version be useful to a reader ?

SPEECH into writing

The best way to see the differences between speech and writing is to turn a piece of speech into written English. These two pages give you practice in doing that.

BROKEN COLLAR BONE

i can remember when i broke my collar bone at east ayton at my old school i was playing leapfrog right and i jumped over this persons shoulder and i landed on my shoulder on the grass and id bust it and i was just screaming my heart out and the and the and the dinner lady was going im sure it isnt that bad now just just just stop screaming and and it will go away and i was er screaming like anything so and i went to the headmasters room and erm i had to lie on this you know settee sort of thing with this blanket over me until my mum came in the car to take me to hospital so i got in the car laying down on the back seat then we got to hospital and i had an xray yes yes it is broken yes broken so they they went and put a sling on me and it was painful so they oh i dont think we should put a sling on it so they went and wrapped this massive bandage all the way round me so it was like that more or less so i couldnt pick anything up cos of cos the bandages were about there and sort of like that so my my my mum had to feed me you know getting all this food in my mouth and to get drinks down me so it was a bit er terrible and then eventually when the bandages came off i could hardly sort of move my arms because i was sort of like that then eventually they started to move me.

What to do
Follow the instructions on the opposite page.
Turn this piece of speech into written English.

1 Dividing it up

Begin by dividing the speech up into sections. These sections will become sentences in the written version. Put a line (/) each time there is a break in the meaning.

> and i was er screaming like anything /so and i went to the headmasters room /and erm i had to lie on this you know settee sort of thing with this blanket over me until my mum came in the car to take me to hospital so i got in the car laying down on the back seat then we got to hospital

> ~~and~~ i was ~~er~~ screaming like anything /so ~~and~~ i went to the headmasters room /~~and erm~~ i had to lie on ~~this you know~~ settee ~~sort of thing~~ with ~~this~~ blanket over me until my mum came in the car to take me to hospital so i got in the car laying down on the back seat then we got to hospital

2 Cutting

Cut out:

ums and ers

repetitions

unnecessary words that make sense in speech but don't make sense in writing (like 'this', or 'and', or 'you know').

3 Changing

Now change the words you have got left so that each section is a proper sentence. You may have to do any of these things:

cut out more words

change the order of the words

add words

When you have finished, each section should read like a proper sentence.

> ~~and~~ i was ~~er~~ screaming like anything /so ~~and~~ i went to the headmasters room /~~and erm~~ i had to lie on ~~this you know~~ settee *a* ~~sort of thing~~ with ~~this~~ *a* blanket over me until my mum came in the car to take me to hospital so i got in the car laying down on the back seat then we got to hospital

> (I) was screaming like anything. (So) (I) went to the headmaster's room. (I) had to lie on a settee with a blanket over me until my mum came in the car to take me to hospital.

4 Punctuating

Now rewrite your sentences, adding the correct punctuation.

Cookery Corner

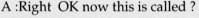

A : Right OK now this is called ?

B : Mediterranean Pork Casserole.

A : What's it got in it?

A : Well, for four people you'll need a pound of pork either cut from the shoulder or the leg; two tablespoons of olive oil; a rounded tablespoon of plain flour; two medium-sized onions which should be sliced and two cloves of garlic; a teaspoon of dried basil and either a pound of tomatoes which you peel and chop or, more simply, a tin of tomatoes; six fluid ounces of wine which can be either white or red; one green pepper and twenty or so um olives, stuffed olives, stuffed with pimento, and salt and freshly milled black pepper.

A : Right, so what do you do?

B : Well, you either need a casserole that you can use on top of the cooker or you can use a frying pan and in this, in the heated olive oil, you fry the cubes of pork...

A : Why?

B : So that they get nice and brown on all sides.

A : All right.

B : You should fry them a few pieces at a time because otherwise it all just gets too juicy and wet.

A : And when you've done that?

B : When you've done that, you take the pork out as you fry it and when all the pork has been fried you add the sliced onions to the casserole and you fry those for a while until they're going brown at the edges. At that stage you put the pork back into the casserole and you add about a rounded tablespoon of plain flour and you stir it in so that all the bits of meat and onion are coated with it.

A : What's the flour for?

B : The flour is so that you get a slightly thicker sauce when the casserole is ready than you would otherwise.

A : Right so you put the flour in, you stir it round, then what happens?

B : Then you pour in the contents of a tin of tomatoes and you stir that around breaking up the tomatoes a bit as you go and add the wine and when it's all bubbling up you take the garlic, the two cloves of garlic which you peel and crush into the mixture and stir.

A : How do you do that ?

B : Well, I've got a garlic crusher. If you haven't then you can just chop it very fine or you can try and flatten it with the blade of a knife and then you put it in.

Scrambled egg with ham and onion

Ingredients

(For 4 people)

6 eggs
4oz. (113g) ham
2 tablespoons of margarine
4 tablespoons of milk
1 medium onion
4 slices freshly made toast
Butter (to spread on the toast)
salt and pepper

1 Chop the onion finely.
2 Break the eggs into a bowl. Beat well and mix in the milk. Season with salt and pepper.
3 Put the margarine into a small saucepan and melt it over a low heat.
4 Add the onion and cook until it is soft.
5 Add the egg mixture and continue to cook on a low heat.
6 Stir with a wooden spoon to stop the egg from sticking.
7 As soon as the egg has set, remove the pan from the heat. Add the ham.
8 Butter the toast and divide the scrambled egg between the four slices.
9 Serve immediately.

Thinking points

1 What are the main differences between the ways in which the two recipes are presented ?

2 Why is this ?

3 Imagine you were writing a recipe for Mediterranean Pork Casserole. How would you write the ingredients down ?

4 Imagine you were explaining on radio or TV how to cook scrambled egg with onion. How would you do it ?

projects

SOUND POEMS

1 Choose a theme for a sound poem like those on pages 38 and 39. Begin by collecting words that will fit into your poem. They may be words from normal speech, or words that you have made up. When you have made a good collection, think about the order in which you are going to describe things. You can then begin to arrange the words you have chosen and build them up into a poem.

2 All the poems in this chapter are meant to be read aloud. You could try making a recording of some of them. This is best done by a small group of people, one of whom is responsible for the recording and nothing else.. You can follow the suggestions on page 41. It is best to have several goes at the recording because what sounds fine to you may not sound so good when it is played back.

summary

WHICH CAME FIRST ?

Speech came before writing, so writing was originally a way of recording language so that it could be read later.

WRITING SOUNDS

Speech is a pattern of sounds. We can use real and invented words to describe and imitate the sounds we hear.

Speech sounds can be divided into consonants and vowels according to the way in which they are made. In English we use the twenty-six letters of the alphabet to write down the sounds of speech.

WEATHER WORDS
SOUND PATTERNS
NIGHT MAIL

Writers can use the words of English (and their own invented words) to imitate and describe the sounds of things they want to describe. This is called onomatopoeia.

WRITING SPEECH DOWN
SPEECH INTO WRITING
COOKERY CORNER

When we write down the exact words someone says it is called a transcript. This has to be changed in a number of ways to turn it into normal written English.

Different *VOICES*

Proverbs

Him a cleber man wha dribe way
hungry just workin him jaw.
De man all honey, fly dem gwine nyam
him up.
Dog-bark neber frightn moon !
Wahn lib a wuk - awks neyga baby !

The twa corbies

As I was walking all alane,
I heard twa corbies making a mane;
The tane unto the tither did say,
'Where sall we gang and dine the day ?'

'In behint yon auld fail dyke,
I wot there lies a new-slain knight;
And nae body kens that he lies there,
But his hawk, his hound, and his lady fair.'

The collier's wife

Somebody's knocking at th' door
  Mother, come down and see.
- I's think it's nobbut a beggar,
  Say I'm busy.

It's not a beggar, mother, - hark
  How 'ard 'e knocks...
- Eh, tha'rt a mard-arsed kid,
  'A'll gi'e thee socks !

English is not just one language that is spoken
in exactly the same way by everyone
everywhere. Different people pronounce it in
different ways and use different words and
different grammar according to who they are
and where they come from.

Making sense

These three texts are in the English spoken by
people from different parts of the world.

1 Can you guess which part of the world for
each one ?

2 Can you work out what each one means ?

51

Accent

People who come from different places pronounce the words of English differently. They may also speak English sentences with a different rhythm and 'tune'. These different ways of pronouncing English are called accents. An accent that belongs to a particular place is called a regional accent.

There is one accent which does not belong to a particular place. It is the accent used by many important and influential people - from politicians to TV news readers. Sometimes people call it a 'posh' accent, but its correct name is Received Pronunciation (or RP for short.)

No one speaks English without an accent: everyone has some kind of accent. No accent is 'better' than any other, but many people find it useful for their work to be able to use the RP accent.

On the tape you will hear the same text read by six people. The first five have regional accents and the sixth speaks RP.

I lived in a small village in the heart of England. We had two cats, but no dog, as my mother would not have dogs. I loved these cats dearly - John, an elderly bachelor of a cat with quiet ways and a wavy tail, and Patsy, a black cat with white paws, white whiskers and a white stomach, very dainty and intelligent, one of the most intelligent animals I've known. She could steal groceries out of bicycle baskets, open pantry and cupboard doors to track down meat, scoop goldfish out of bowls, and, after a hunting spree in the fields, would line up her little dormice and vole victims exactly in order of size, the longest first, in the porch, to greet whoever was coming in. A mathematical cat, perhaps ? She also caught rabbits, and, later on, when food rationing grew tight, my mother would cook these

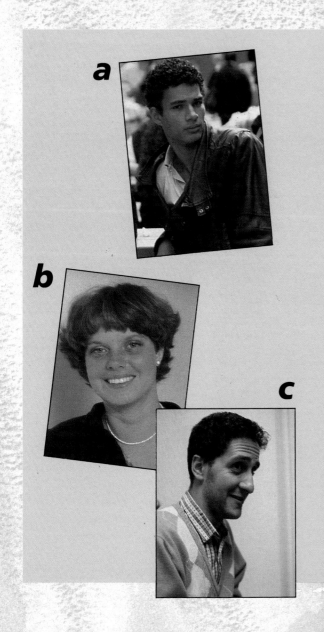

WORDS

As you listen to the readings, try to pick out particular words that the speakers pronounce differently. Here are some suggestions:

heart	ways	whiskers
baskets	vole	mother

RHYTHM AND TUNE

Can you notice any differences in the way the speakers read whole sentences ? Do they give them a different rhythm, or a different 'tune' ?

CLARITY AND PREFERENCE

1 Which of the readings did you find easiest to follow ?

2 Why do you think this was ?

3 Which of them did you like the sound of best and why ?

rabbits, though she did not tell us at the time in case it put us off. I can remember my brother scoffing rabbit pie with relish, then suddenly looking round the table and exclaiming in a horrified voice, for five of the family were eating rabbit legs with fingers and gusto, especially my father, never a dainty eater -

'We're eating a deformed rabbit ! It's got five legs !'

No, dear,' answered my mother placidly. 'There are two rabbits.'

I knew where she'd got the second one from, because I'd been there when Patsy had carried it home in triumph. But we didn't tell.

Gene Kemp : Dog days and cat naps

Dialect 1

In many different parts of Britain and around the world, people speak different versions of English. These different versions are called dialects. You can spot different dialects by the words they use and the ways in which words are arranged into sentences.

What words do you use ?

1 Look at the games being played in the pictures. How many of them can you recognise ?

2 What name do you give to each of the games ?

3 In most games you are allowed to be 'out' of the game for a moment. (For example if your shoe is coming off and you need to stop to put it on.) To do this you usually have to say a special word. What word or words do you use ?

4 The words for the game and the special words for having a break are different in different dialects. The map and the list show some of the different words that are used. How many of them have you heard before ? Are there any words that you know which are not there ?

catch
chain
he
it
stag
tag
tick
tig
touch

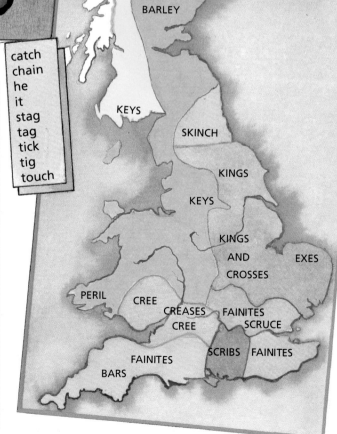

BARLEY

KEYS

SKINCH

KINGS

KEYS

KINGS
AND   EXES
CROSSES

PERIL

CREE

CREASES   FAINITES
CREE   SCRUCE

SCRIBS   FAINITES

FAINITES

BARS

PROBLEMS

Naturally people like their own dialect: they feel at home with it and speak it with their friends and family. But if we only had our regional dialects we might find it difficult when we travelled around the country.

1 Why are the children in these pictures arguing ?

2 Look at the maps again. Are there any words that the children in the pictures could have used which would be understood anywhere in the country ?

STANDARD ENGLISH

There is a dialect of English which can be understood anywhere in the United Kingdom. It is called Standard English.

Dialect phrase book

Try writing your own dialect phrase book.

1 Make a list of all the words and expressions you can think of that are special to your local dialect. Here are some suggestions:

- Greetings (what you say to people when you meet them.)

- Forms of address (what you call people, apart from their names.)

- Words for games

- The word you use for food you eat in the middle of the morning.

- Words for size (to say something is very big or very small)

2 Write out your words in a list.

3 Against each one write what it would be in Standard English.

Dialect 2

VOCABULARY AND GRAMMAR

The easiest way to spot different dialects is through the special words they use: through their vocabulary. Dialects can also differ in the way sentences are made up: in their grammar. This is harder to spot, but it's just as important.

I live on a green. It's a slope. There's houses everywhere: all the sides apart from one way where you go in. And we play football there during the summer and when it rains we still play football and we've mucked a bit of the green up. And we slip and we've put one large window through and since then we haven't been able to play. And we can't come up on to the school field afterwards for have a game because there'll be a policeman patrolling in a car. And we just haven't got the facilities to play.

The parts that have been highlighted are not Standard English.

Dialect	Standard English
There's	There are
We've put one large window through	We've broken one large window
We can't come up ...for have a game	We can't come up to have a game

WRITTEN STANDARD ENGLISH

I live on a green. It's a slope. There are houses everywhere: on all the sides apart from where you go in. We play football there during the summer. When it rains we still play football and we've cut a bit of the green up. We slip and we've broken one large window. Since then we haven't been able to play. We can't come up on to the school field afterwards to have a game because there will be a policeman patrolling in a car. We just haven't got the facilities to play.

$\mathcal{W}ee$ beasties

TRANSCRIPT

And I do a lot of school work - I go to the schools and - and talk to the bairns at the schools about wildlife natural history then - and - conservation and we take - walks and go oot with the kiddies/the teachersll phone up and say right were going to the seashore/is it possible to come wi us and we gone and gone to the seashore and go in the rock pools say for instance now turn over the stanes in the rock pools and - and hunt for all the wee beasties that bides underneath them - you know/the big important thing is to get the kids to understand to put the stones back again because youre taking away a habitat if you leave them - over - overturned

PUNCTUATED SPEECH

And I do a lot of school work. I go to the schools and talk to the bairns at the school about wildlife, natural history and conservation and we take walks and go oot with the kiddies. The teachers'll phone up and say, 'Right we're going to the seashore. Is it possible to come wi us ?' And we gone and gone to the seashore and go in the rock pools, say. For instance now turn over the stanes in the rock pools and hunt for all the wee beasties that bides underneath them, you know. The big important thing is to get the kids to understand to put the stones back again, because you're taking away a habitat if you leave them overturned.

What to do

1 Copy and complete this table.

2 Now write a Standard Written English version of what he says.

Dialect	Standard English
bairns	
oot	
wi	
gone and gone	
stanes	
wee beasties	
that bides	
understand to	

Standard English

When do people use a local dialect and when do they use Standard English ?

1

2

3

4

5

6

The pictures on this page show different situations in which people are speaking. Look at each one carefully and then answer these questions.

1 What is happening ?

2 What are the people talking about ?

3 Should they be speaking Standard English or a regional dialect ? Why ?

4 What would people think if they chose to speak differently ? (For example, Standard English instead of regional dialect.)

TELLING THE TALE

Suppose you were one of the girls in the
pictures. You might tell the story of what
happened to you differently according
to the person you were talking to.

In pairs

Act two conversations:

1 The girl explains (in local dialect) to her best
friend what happened.

2 The girl explains (in Standard English) to the
headteacher of the school what happened.

Writing

Now write it as a story (in Standard English).
Write it as if you were the girl, describing
something that had happened to you.

NARROW ESCAPE

A: His parachute collapsed because he - he come above me/cos when youre descending you leave a partial vacuum above your chute/now - he come above me/and therefore there was very little air which collapsed his chute and that caused him to slip in through my rigging lines/all of a sudden I found meself engulfed in a green - a green blanket of nylon which I automatically grabbed and I twigged on exactly what the situation was/held me equipment/ shouted to him to drop his and pull for his reserve - but - he panicked a bit/ he switched off and so I had to hold him - cos the danger was now if I hadve let him go - it - his canopy couldve pulled - on to mine and it could have nearly collapsed and give me a total malfunction of mine and which wouldve both put both up the creek so - er - I just kept a hold as hard as I could/kept me equipment on which in that position I had to do because if Id have dropped it I wouldve hit him/might have killed him/and we took the best landing we could

B: So you came down on the one parachute

A: Yes on my parachute/and this all happened in the space of what - ten or twelve seconds - and it you know it just happened that fast there was ney time to think/just had to get on and dey the job and that was it/there - there was basically no time to panic no time for feelings/had all me feelings afterwards -like- this situation we had been lectured/youve got to accept the fact that youre ganna break something/I knew that straight away just hoped to god it wasnt me neck and it wasnt/the container that I was holding hit the back of me leg - and smashed the leg in three places the tib and fib end and broke the skin/the leg was out and when I landed I also crushed a vertebrae in me spine/and thats - thats whats give us really me most trouble that

B: Do you actually remember hitting the ground

A: No at that moment I was away every way but soon as I hit the ground it blanked you know/ -but er the pain woke us up

B:How do you feel now that youve learned youre going to get this award

A:Great/just takes all the pain out of it/all that/this has been six months in plaster and another three month to gan /its just fantastic

B:But do you think you will jump again

A:Its a hell of a question/I dont know/thats ganna take more guts than what it took to get up there in the first place that/so well have a good lang think about that

Thinking about what he said

1 What impressions did you get of this man from what he said and the way he said it ?

2 Listen carefully to the tape and study the transcript.Then make a list of the main things that happened as the two parachutists came down.

Telling the story

Use the information and ideas in the conversation to tell the story of what happened. Write as if you were the person it happened to, but write in Standard English, not a regional dialect.

Looking at the dialect.

Some of the dialect words have been marked. So have parts of sentences that use a different grammar from Standard English. Write each one down, and against it write what it would be in Standard English.

LAUNCHING *the lifeboat*

A: Im sure you remember the old lifeboat

B: Oh yes yes / she used to be kept up close to the school / and its a very narrow street to bring her down / there used to be four men I think - on the wheels - with big props of wood helping her down and then shifting her around and there was anywhere from 20 to 35 men catching hold of the ropes to ease her down - and I think the boat and the carriage was ten ton weight - all the lot / and there was one incident when - er - we was bringing her down / she got down the road all right / going out on practice - not - she woodnt called out for rescue work she was on practice / and there was a - er - there was a young man in front of me / called Mitchell / lived over in Scarrick Hill / and he tripped over a stone - a boulder / he fell in front of the big wheel not the small wheel and the wheel hit the stone and went right over his body / never broke a bone / but it bruised un and he was in bed for several weeks / then he got all right again / if the wheel had went over un on the side hedve been squashed to a pulp / twas ten ton going over his body / well it frightened the life of me out you know / well we used to - the fastest we got that boat down I think was four minutes / and er I didn used to go out in her every time / sometimes I used to go out in her for practice / I been out - I been out re- / I been out doing rescue work in her as well because I woodn always home and I woodn always wanted to go out / because - er - if - er - when the rocket went up you would all run up to the lifeboat / you would - you would - er - you would snap a badge or the coxswain would give you a badge to put on / well that would be the crew / theyd jump aboard and then - or get their oilskins and help her down the road and when she got - just before she got afloat wed jump

...aboard and off/but the other men they had badges all issued out and they would help her down the road and help her up again/now I think they used to get in they days three and six a man for - helping/it used to take a long time to get her up - out of the water and - now weve got a inshore rescue boat which is doing good work/shes doing good work

Thinking about the story

Listen carefully to the tape and then answer these questions.

1 Where was the lifeboat kept ?

2 What was involved in launching it ?

3 Who used to launch it ?

4 How long did it take ?

5 What happened to Mitchell ?

6 How did the lifeboatmen know when they were needed ?

7 What did they do when there was an emergency ?

8 What kind of lifeboat have they got now ?

Writing

Imagine that you are writing for a local newspaper and have just interviewed this speaker. Write a short article about his memories based on what he said.

Studying the dialect

Some of the dialect words have been marked. So have parts of sentences that use a different grammar from Standard English. Write each one down, and against it write what it would be in Standard English. See if you can find any other examples of dialect words and sentences and do the same with these.

summary

ACCENT
This is the way in which people pronounce words and sentences. A regional accent is one which is used by people who come from a particular area.

RECEIVED PRONUNCIATION (RP)
This accent does not belong to a particular area. It is used throughout the United Kingdom. It is the accent of many people in business, politics, television and radio. Some people use RP instead of their regional accent because they think it is better and will help them in their work.

DIALECTS
Language comes in different forms. These are called dialects. Regional dialects are spoken in a particular area. They can differ from each other in two main ways.

Dialect differences

1. Vocabulary

Different dialects use special words and expressions which are not used in other dialects. Examples of this are the words snap, bait, and snack, which all mean the same thing in different parts of England.

2. Grammar

Dialects also differ in the way they arrange words to make sentences. For example in some dialects people say 'it had went', while in others they say 'it had gone'.

STANDARD ENGLISH
Speakers of one dialect may find it difficult to understand another dialect. There is one dialect that is understood throughout Britain. It is called Standard English. Many people speak Standard English at work and with people from outside their own area. It is normally used for writing. Standard English can be spoken with any accent.

5 The right word in the place

What you say and how you say it depend on three main things:

You can quickly see how this works if you look at what happens when things go wrong.

Topic	**What** you are talking about.
Audience	**Who** you are talking to.
Purpose	**Why** you are talking to them.

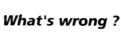

What's wrong ?

Clearly these people are not using language in the way we would expect them to.

1 What is wrong with the way in which each person is speaking ?

2 What do you think each person should be saying ?

SWEET TALKING

Each of these people is talking about sweets. As you can see from their faces they have different opinions about them. In each picture the topic is the same, but the audience and the purpose are different. What do you think each one is saying?

1 Look at each picture carefully.

2 Look at the lists of words on this page. Choose some words from the lists that you think the person might use in that situation. Try to think of other words that they might use.

3 Write down what you think the person is saying. Use as many of your chosen words as you can.

cloying	bite	aniseed ball	amber
creamy	bolt	barley sugar	black
delicious	chew	bonbon	blue
disgusting	chomp	candy	bronze
foul	crunch	caramel	brown
horrible	devour	chew	buff
juicy	enjoy	chocolate	cherry-red
luscious	gnaw	confectionery	chestnut
moreish	gulp down	gob-stopper	creamy
nauseous	guzzle	gum	crimson
nice	lick	humbug	dark
overpowering	make short work of	liquorice	emerald
repulsive	masticate	lollipop	gold
revolting	munch	lolly	green
rich	nibble	marshmallow	khaki
scrumptious	peck	mint	mahogany
sickly	rend	nougat	mauve
spicy	savour	pear drop	milky
succulent	scrunch	sweetmeat	mud-coloured
sugary	suck	toffee	mushroom
sweet	swallow		orange
unpleasant	tear		pink
velvety	wolf		purple
vile			red
yukky			scarlet
yummy			silvery
			white
			yellow

SPARKLE. DON'T FIZZ.

itrus Spring from Britvic.
refreshing blend of sparkling
water and pure fruit juice, with
rtificial colours, sweeteners,
rings or preservatives.
ere are three delicious flavours
ose from, so take your pick: Lime,
or Orange.

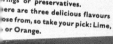

5P OFF 9 900350 25005 *Citrus Spring*

Tip it

Whip it **Pour it**

Carnation DESSERT TOP Skimmed Milk with Non-Milk Fat

Snip it!

A rich creamy topping made for whipping or pouring to
reate a smooth tasting treat you will want to eat again
nd again.
And the great news is Carnation Dessert Top has over a

third less fat than double cream
with far fewer calories. Snip out your
coupons and treat your family today.
Can help slimming or weight control only as part of a calorie controlled diet.

Advertising

When you make up an advertisement, you have
to choose your words very carefully. Look at the
way in which the advertisements on this page
use words and pictures to sell their products.

1 How would you describe the topic of each
advert ?

2 What is the purpose of each one ?

3 What kind of audience is each one aimed at ?

Advertising Sweets

TOFFEE CHEWS

Making up an advert

You are the head of a sweet company and you
are going to market a new sweet.

1 Decide what kind of sweet you want to start
selling. Think about exactly what it will look
and taste like.

2 Decide on the kind of person you want to
sell it to - small children ? adults ? teenagers ?

3 Think of a good name for your sweet. Try to
find one that will make it sound really
attractive.

4 Think about how you will advertise your new
product - what kind of words and pictures
will you use ?

5 Now make up an advertisement for your new
sweet.

Advertising Sweets

1st crook :('posh' accent): I say ! 'Midget Gems. I haven't seen those in years.

Boss : Genuine of course. Trebor.

2nd crook : 'Course they're perishin' genuine.

1st crook : Fine specimens. I can offer you 6 bags of mint creams.

People who make up advertisements have to keep on thinking up new ideas. Often they base their adverts on characters or stories or films that they think people like. Look at this TV advert and then answer the questions.

Boss : I think we're talking Sherbet Lemons.

1st crook :Yeah yeah of course. I'll up the ante to 3 bags of jelly beans...and I'll throw in the Top Cream Toffees.

Boss : Excellent !

2nd crook : No tricks, mind...or Tiny can turn ugly.

Voice over : Trebor Tantalisers : just the job.

Questions

1 What kind of film is this advert based on ?

2 In the original film, what would the crooks have been talking about ?

3 What's the point of advertising sweets in this way ?

4 What age group is it aimed at ?

5 Do you think it works ? What are your reasons ?

Writing

1 Write a short script showing how this sort of scene would have gone in the original film.

2 Try writing a short TV advert of your own. Choose a product from list A and a style from list B.

A

junior fashions

mint ice cream

bicycle

B

Grange Hill, or a similar school 'soap'

an American police film

a news broadcast

WRITING ABOUT SCHOOL MEALS

These descriptions of school meals are all by people still at school. Read them and answer the questions at the bottom of the page.

At school we have a choice for dinner and a choice for pudding. The choice for dinner was cheese rounders and baked beans or minced pork and mash. The choice for pudding was chocolate crunch or Fairy cakes. I don't have school dinners because I don't like them. I have packed lunch instead. Today I had a packet of spring onion crisps a banana a twirl and a bottle of strawberry cream soda. Five people have packed lunch and twenty people have school dinners.

Nigel Farish

Open Monday to Friday, the Kyle Academy dinner hall offers a variety of foods at extremely reasonable prices, in fact at one extremely reasonable price: 67p. The menu changes daily, but some things in life always remain constant - chips and thick custard are represented without fail. The cooks will be gratified to learn that their practice has paid off: the chips are of consistently high quality and there is nothing wrong with the custard which ten seconds in a microwave wouldn't cure. Lasagne, spaghetti bolognaise and sausages are frequently recurring fare and as such are satisfactory, while the meat pies (which meat we are never told) are unfortunately disastrous.

Nicholas Barber

When we enter in the restaurant to lunch we could smell the delicious dinner waiting for us. We add the estomac empty. The servant served us. We add 3 courses for £1.00. First the salad then the desert and next the meat. They had a skate under their feet to served us. Delicious.

Wesse Sebastien

What to do

1 One of the writers is 17, one is 9, and one is 10 and French. Which was which ?

2 Have a look at the writing by the French child. Make a list of all the points that made you realise who wrote it. For each one explain what the writer meant to say. (And before you start feeling too superior, just try writing about your school meals in French !)

3 Now compare the other two pieces of writing. How can you tell that the writer of one of them is much older ? Think about these things:

a) words (length, how 'technical', how varied.)

b) sentences (how long, how varied, how complicated.)

3 Now try writing about school meals yourself. Write two short pieces:

a) a description that conveys your own thoughts and feelings about school food.

b) the script for a TV advert for school meals (it could be based on the gangster idea used by Trebor, or a new idea of your own.)

Sweet tooth

HAVE YOU A SWEET TOOTH?

To find out, answer each of the questions, tick the appropriate one, then check your score, pals!

A

1 It's breakfast time, and Mum says the choice of menu is all yours. Do you. . .
A. Have yoghurt, fruit juice and brown-bread toast?
B. Choose toast with jam, and tea with two sugars?
C. Decide on bread with golden syrup followed by chocolate bickies and a cup of sugar with just a drop of tea in it?

2 Teacher announces the dentist is calling next week. Do you. . .
A. Try and cut down on sticky sweets?
B. Get so worried about the state of your teeth you eat even more sweets to comfort yourself?
C. Not worry at all because your teeth are in perfect condition.

3 You are about to enter the swimming pool. Do you. . .
A. Drape yourself in a big towel, as the others always make jokes about hippos coming for a bathe?
B. Stride confidently forward knowing you look trim and fit?
C. Tell yourself your swimming costume must keep shrinking, 'cos it gets tighter every time you wear it?

4 Your sister brings home an iced cake that she's made in her cookery class. Do you. . .
A. Avoid it like the plague since it looks a mess anyway?
B. Risk a slice because you like cake?
C. Wait 'til she's left the room and then scoff most of the cake, telling yourself you've got to give it a fair trial?

TURN THE PAGE TO CHECK YOUR SCORE

Can you believe how much sugar is in your weekly shopping basket!

The percentages show the approximate sugar content of the types of foods illustrated.

57% **SUGAR WHEAT PUFFS**

54% INSTANT WHIP

15% ICE CREAM

Tempting! Until you realise it contains approximately 12 teaspoonsful of sugar.

22% TOMATO KETCHUP

23% BROWN SAUCE

75% DRINKING CHOCOLATE

1% SOUP

4% BAKED BEANS

33% Chocolate BISCUITS

68% JAM

Remember:
Sugar+Plaque
=Acids
=Tooth Decay

61% Blackcurrant DRINK

98% BOILED SWEETS

90% DOLLY MIXTURE

66% LEMON CURD

Have you ever considered the effect your diet has on your teeth? Brushing your teeth will go a long way towards controlling tooth decay and gum disease. However, it is equally important to cut down the amount of sugar you eat and, especially, how often you eat or drink it.

Plaque is a sticky layer of germs which lives on your teeth and gums. Sugar, from the food you eat, reacts with plaque to produce acids which cause tooth decay and gum disease. Every time you eat or drink sugar your teeth are subject to an acid attack of about half an hour.

Plaque begins to re-form 20 or 30 seconds after you have removed it from your teeth and gums during tooth-brushing. Sugar is the enemy. Cut it out and you'll cut down your tooth decay and gum disease.

Sugar is not essential for energy. It can lead to tooth decay and the calories it contains can make you fat. Sugar contains no other nutrients at all. And yet an average of 80lbs of sugar is consumed per person per year!

It is unrealistic to presume that you can cut sugar out of your diet altogether. However, to reduce acid attack you should restrict your sugar consumption to mealtimes.

If you want to eat in between meals choose unsweetened snacks and drinks, like cheese, fresh fruit, fresh vegetables, nuts, wholemeal bread, natural yoghurt, wholegrain cereals, fresh milk, unsweetened fruit juices, or low calorie drinks. And cut out sugar in tea and coffee.

Sweets and sweet biscuits are full of sugar, and there are also lots of foods which, surprisingly, contain 'hidden sugar'.

Make sure that you read the labels on tins and packets carefully before you buy them – you'll be surprised how often sugar is there. The higher on the list of ingredients sugar appears the higher the proportion there is of it. And it won't always say 'sugar', it might say 'sucrose', 'dextrose', 'fructose', 'glucose', 'maltose'.

What to do

Answer these questions for A and B. In each case explain as fully as you can why you have given that answer.

1 What is the subject of the writing ?

2 What is its purpose ?

3 At what age group is it aimed ?

4 At what kind of person is it aimed ?

Now answer these questions about both texts:

1 Which one contains the most information ?

2 Which is more enjoyable to read ?

3 Which is easier to read and why ?

4 What could be done to improve them ?

Writing

Suppose you had to explain to a five-year-old about the connection between what we eat and what happens to our teeth. How would you do it ? Write it as a conversation between a mother and her child. Start like this:

MOTHER : No. You mustn't eat sweets between meals.

CHILD : Why not ?

0–4
You are too aware of your looks and your sparkling teeth to eat lots of sweet things.

5–10
Average. You do try to eat less sweets and sticky puddings because you've got enough fillings as it is, but it's a hard struggle.

11–20
Oh, dear! You have more gaps in your gums than teeth. You eat at least one cream cake per day, and are probably eating a sweet while you're reading this.

1. A–0, B–2, C–5; 2. A–3, B–5, C–0; 3. A–5, B–0, C–3; 4. A–0, B–2, C–5.

71

Special words

Special subjects need special words. If two car mechanics are talking to each other, they use the correct words to describe parts of a car:

It isn't just specialists who have to use such words. We all use them from time to time. They save a lot of time and help us avoid a lot of mistakes. Look at the picture below and then answer the questions.

Questions

1 What is the correct name for each of the labelled items ? Write the letter of the label, followed by the name.

2 Suppose you had to describe each of these things to a young child who didn't know the correct word for it. What would you call each one ? (You may find that you have to use rather more words than you did before.)

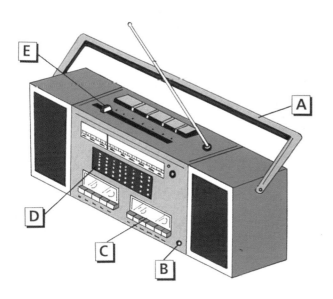

Getting it taped

1 What is the correct name for each of the labelled parts of the stereo radio-cassette ? If you don't know them, try to choose the correct word from the list at the bottom of the page.

2 Suppose you were describing this machine to someone who had never seen or heard one. How would you explain what each of these things was for ?

Bits of a bike

Now do the same with this diagram of a bike:

1 Give the correct special word (or use the list at the bottom of this page to help you.)

2 Make up a description that would describe this part of the bike to someone who doesn't know the special word.

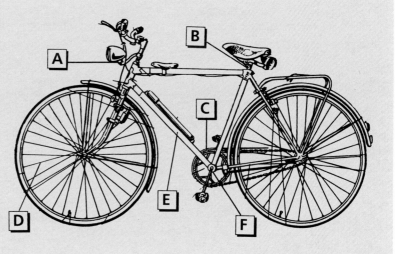

Words

The list that follows contains all the words for the stereo radio-cassette and bicycle diagrams. It also contains a number of other words. They are the special words from four other subjects.

1 Copy out all the words that don't belong to stereos and bicycles.

2 Divide them into four lists according to their special subjects.

3 Choose one of the lists and explain what you think each of the special words means.

Clue : each of your lists should contain five words

beam	carrying handle	cello	chain guard	chain wheel
clarinet	lamp bracket	depth gauge	diving mask	down tube
graphic equaliser	sepal	flipper	forward roll	recorder
seat pillar	stamen	microphone socket	petal	spoke
stalk	vault	snorkel	somersault	trampoline
trombone	volume control	stigma	tambourine	wet suit
fast forward button				

Sweet dreams

BEFORE YOU START

Before starting work on this unit, think about these questions:

1 How much do you know about dreaming ?

2 Do you dream a lot ?

3 What sort of things do you dream about ?

4 Do you find it easy to remember your dreams ?

5 Do you understand where your dreams come from or what they mean ?

6 Have you read anything about dreaming ?

7 If so, what kind of writing was it ? Scientific ? Fiction ? In a book ? In a magazine ?

8 Have you been told anything about dreaming ? If so, what kind of telling ? Chat ? A lesson ? On TV or radio ?

In this unit we look at different kinds of writing about dreaming. Read the texts and then look at the activities at the bottom of page 75.

A

Dreaming
Scientists do not yet understand why and how we dream. It could be that the brain is sorting out its filing system.

When you are asleep, you are not conscious of the world around you but your brain is still at work. You are thinking and feeling things which you sometimes remember as dreams. No one really knows why we dream. Some people think that the brain is helping us to sort out information. Others think that brain cells are being repaired.

WHEN YOU SLEEP

When you are asleep, you become unconscious for a time and the cortex works far more slowly than when you are awake.

There are several kinds of sleep. When you are in the lightest phase of sleep, you often dream. This phase is called R.E.M. (Rapid Eye Movement) because during it, your eyes move backwards and forwards rapidly under closed eyelids. This usually happens just before you wake up. When you are most deeply asleep, growth hormones are released into your blood.

Sleep is important because it gives your body time to grow and repair itself. It also gives your brain time to sort out all of its experiences. There is still a lot that is not understood about sleep and dreaming.

Brain waves

There is special equipment that can detect 'brain waves' (electrical activity in the brain) and print them out as a pattern to show what is happening when people are awake and asleep. The equipment is called an electroencephalograph machine. ▼

BRAIN WAVES

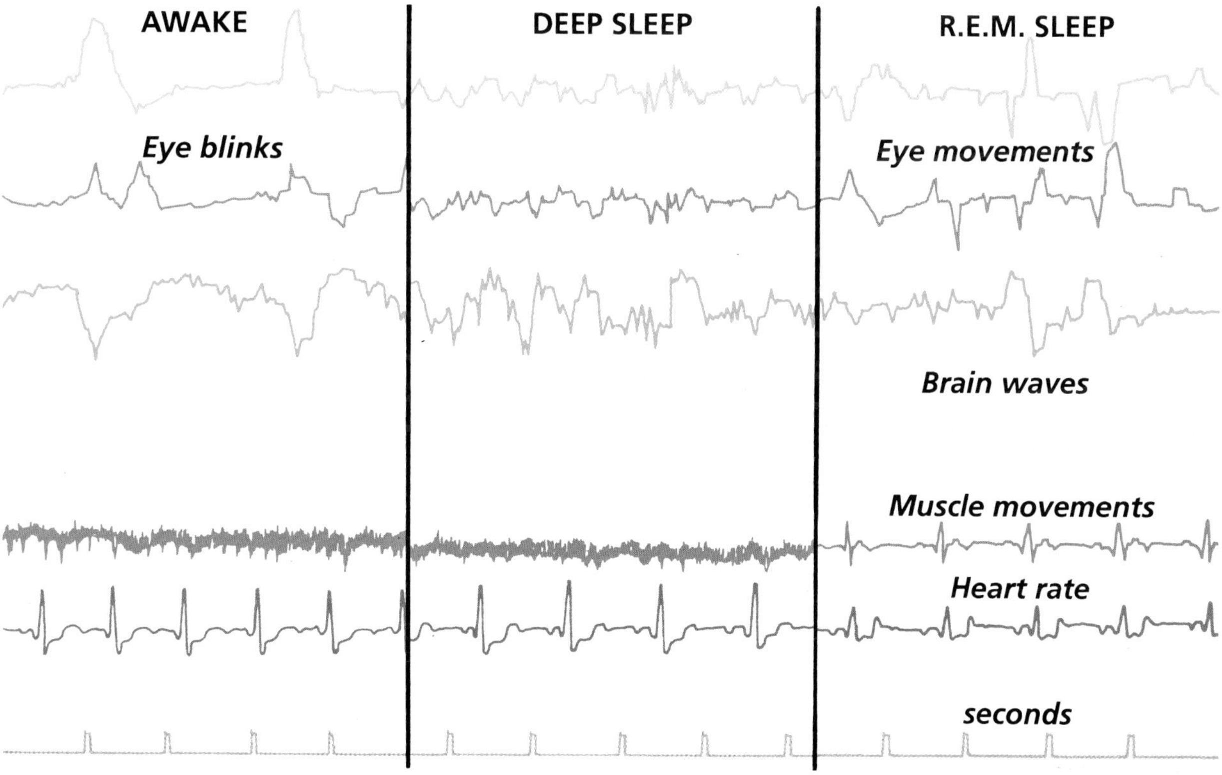
AWAKE
DEEP SLEEP
R.E.M. SLEEP
Eye blinks
Eye movements
Brain waves
Muscle movements
Heart rate
seconds

What to do

Compare A and B.

1 How much information do you get from each illustration ?

2 How much information do you get from each piece of writing ?

3 List the special words about sleep and dreaming that each writer uses.

4 Which text is more difficult to read and understand ? Why ?

5 Both writers try to explain why we dream. Do they agree ?

6 Look back at your answers so far. How would you describe the audience for each text. What are your reasons ?

marianne's dream

Marianne was ill. To while away the time in bed she did some drawing.

She drew, as she nearly always did, a house. A house with four windows and a front door. The walls were not quite straight, because she wasn't ruling the lines, and the chimney was a little large. Over the chimney she drew a faint scribble of smoke.

She drew a fence round the house, and a path leading from the front door to a gate. She put some flowers inside the fence, and all around she drew long scribbly grass, which she hoped would be waist high at least. In the grass outside the fence she drew a few large rough-looking stones or lumps of rock, like those she had seen on the moors in Cornwall.

Marianne was no child prodigy at drawing. Like so many of us, she had often had ideas that if she had a particular set of coloured pencils, this tiny paintbox, or that very thick black pencil, she would suddenly find herself able to reproduce on paper the pictures she could see so clearly in her mind's eye. But somehow the magic never worked; and though this pencil had seemed to hold out the same sort of promise, her house looked as much like a shaky doll's house, and her grass as little like anything growing, as ever.

Later that day, Marianne fell asleep.

Marianne dreamed.

She was in a great open stretch of country, flat like a prairie, covered, as far as she could see, with the long dry grass in which she was standing more than knee deep. There were no roads, no paths, no hills and no valleys. Only the prairie stretched before her on all sides till it met the grey encircling sky. Here and there it was dotted with great stones or rocks, which rose just above the level of the tall grass, like heads peering from all directions.

Marianne stood and looked. There seemed to be nothing to do and nowhere to go. Wherever she looked she saw nothing but grass and sky, the same on every side of her. Yet something, a nagging uneasiness which she could not account for, drove her to start walking; and because at one point on the skyline she thought she could see something like a faint trickle of smoke, she walked towards that.

The ground under her feet was rutted and uneven, and the grass harsh and prickling. She could not move fast, and it seemed that she had walked a long way before she saw that she had been right about the faint line in the sky. It was a wavering stream of smoke, rising in the windless air from the chimney of a house.

It was a curious looking house, with leaning walls, its windows and door blank and shut. It rose unexpectedly straight from the prairie: a low uneven fence separated its small plot from the surrounding ground, though the coarse grass was the same within and without. There were some large pale yellow flowers about, which Marianne could not recognize, growing a foot or two high; they seemed to be as much outside the fence as in, and certainly did not constitute a garden. Nothing moved except the thread of smoke rising from the chimney.

In all that vast expanse nothing else moved.

There was a gate in the fence. Marianne pushed it open and walked up the path to the door. She did not much like the look of the house, with its blank staring windows and its bare front door, but she liked the prairie even less.

'I must get in,' said Marianne aloud in her dream. 'I've got to get in.'

There was no knocker and there was no bell. Marianne knocked with her knuckles, but it was a disappointing little noise and she was not surprised that no one answered. She looked around for a stone to beat on the door but the only stones were the great grey boulders outside the fence. As she stood, considering what to do, she heard the distant sound of wind. Across the prairie it blew towards her, and in its path the grass whistled and rustled, dry stalk on dry stalk, and bent, so that she could see the path of the wind as it approached her. Then it was all around her, and everything that had been so still before became alive with movement. The grass writhed and tore at its roots, the pale flowers beat against their stems, the thin thread of smoke was blown out like a candle flame, and disappeared into the dark sky. The wind whistled round the house and was gone, leaving Marianne deaf for a moment, and suddenly chilled.

'I'm frightened here,' she said. 'I've got to get away from the grass and the stones and the wind. I've got to get into the house.'

No voice spoke in reply to her words, and there was no signal from the silent house; but she knew the answer as if she had heard it.

'I could get in,' Marianne thought, 'if there was a person inside the house. There has got to be a person. I can't get in unless there is somebody there.'

'Why isn't there someone in the house?' she cried to the empty world around her.

'Put someone there,' the silent answer said.

'How can I?' Marianne protested. 'How can I put someone in the house? I can't get in myself! And I've got to get in!' she heard herself say, and the words woke her up. With difficulty she struggled back to realise that the house and prairie were gone: she was lying in bed, and the memory of the six weeks more to be spent there was lying in wait for her, to weigh down her spirits as soon as she was sufficiently awake to remember.

What to do

1 Read again the description of the house that Marianne drew. Draw what she drew.

2 Now look at the description of the house that she saw in her dream. Draw what she saw.

3 Compare your two drawings - are they the same, or different ?

4 Compare the two descriptions. How do they differ ? Why do you think that is ?

5 The writer of this story has her own ideas about dreams. How do these come out in her writing ? Are they like the ideas in the other texts ?

6 What age group do you think this story is written for and why ?

Your writing

You are going to write two short descriptions of dreams - for different audiences.

1 The first is for people of your own age. Either think of a particular dream that you have had yourself, or make one up. Then describe it as vividly as you can, so that someone of your own age would enjoy reading it.

2 Now describe the same dream so that a child of five would understand it. (You may also need to think about whether your audience would find the dream frightening. If so, how will you alter it to make it less frightening ?)

Local radio trainee reporter exercise

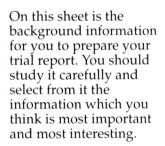

On this sheet is the background information for you to prepare your trial report. You should study it carefully and select from it the information which you think is most important and most interesting.

Remember : you are the person who has gathered this information. You were there. So if you need to add small details to your report to give it 'colour' - that's fine, provided you don't go against any of the information on this sheet.

Remember too : radio is a live medium. Our listeners don't want to hear someone reading a newspaper report. Make it live !

FIRE AT BRUNSWICKS DEPARTMENT STORE

Brunswicks is a large department store in the centre of town. It is a local landmark. The fire broke out in the fashion and furs department at about midnight last night. Local fire chief Station Officer Weston has confirmed that the sprinkler system failed to work allowing fire to sweep through the entire floor, soon spreading to other floors.

Firemen and fire engines were called in from several local fire stations. Altogether there were six fire engines. The firemen worked throughout the night, but were unable to save the store. But they did manage to stop the fire spreading to other stores.

This morning the fire is out and Brunswicks is a smoking ruin. Because the fire happened at night, there was no one on the premises, except for the nightwatchman, Dave Haskins (57). When interviewed, he said, 'I was patrolling on the floor above, when I smelled smoke. I went down to the furs department and the whole place was already ablaze. There was nothing I could do except dial 999.'

Local police are already working on the theory that this may be a case of arson. Chief Inspector James ('Lucky') Mann said, 'We have to follow up all lines of enquiry, but it does look as if this fire could have been started deliberately.' But he wouldn't comment on the possibility that the fire was the work of animal rights activists. Similar fires have been started by incendiary bombs in a number of similar stores over the past two years.

These are the beginnings of some of the tapes which were submitted.

Angela McGee

A serious fire broke out in a local Department store, Brunswicks, at about midnight last night. The fire started in the fashion and furs department, but it soon took hold and spread rapidly.

Firemen and appliances from a number of local stations were called to the fire, but they were unable to prevent the fire completely destroying the store. Apparently the fire spread so fast because the store's sprinkler system failed to work.

Fortunately no one was hurt, because the store was closed for the night. The only person on the premises was the nightwatchman, Mr D.Haskins. He discovered the fire during the course of his regular patrol, but was unable to do anything except summon the emergency services...

Mark Dakin

A well known landmark in the centre of town has been completely destroyed by fire. Brunswicks Department Store, used by thousands of shoppers every week was completely gutted when fire swept through the five storey building.

I visited the site early this morning and spoke to Station Officer Weston who is in charge of the team of firemen fighting the blaze. He told me that although the store was fitted with sprinklers, for some reason these failed to work and the fire soon took hold. As a result there was nothing to prevent the flames spreading rapidly and engulfing the whole building.

As I stood looking at the scene of ruin and devastation I spoke to the night watchman Dave Haskins. Dave's 57 and has worked at Brunswicks for 23 years. He told me...

Hal Charters

Well it was certainly a hot night in the old town last night ! Multi-million pound superstore Brunswicks went up like the proverbial tinderbox, when someone put a match to the fashion department. Who that someone was the police aren't saying, but when I tell you that the fire started in the fur department, and that those animal rights freedom fighters have been active in the area recently, it doesn't take much intelligence to put two and two together.

I heard about the blaze first thing this morning, so I thought I'd get straight down there and give things the once over. Of course the action was really over by then - just smoking rubble and charred timber - some barbecue ! But I just managed to catch a few words with Dave Haskins. Dave's the nightwatchman at Brunswicks and he was pretty cut up about things as you can imagine. Still I managed to get him to say a few words...

1 Read the details of the competition, and then the three tapes. Which of the three do you think is the best and why ?

2 How would you have tackled the report ? Read the information sheet again and make up your own report for the competition. (If you have a cassette recorder you could try recording it too.)

summary

SWEET TALKING
We select different words according to the person we are speaking to (or writing for) and according to the effect we want to have on them - even when the subject is the same.

ADVERTISING SWEETS
Advertisers sometimes sell their products by borrowing the language and style of other topics. For example one TV advert for sweets is based on old gangster films and treats the sweets as if they were stolen jewels.

WRITING ABOUT SCHOOL MEALS
We can judge the age and experience of writers by the words and sentences they use, especially if we compare what they write about the same topic.

SWEET TOOTH
Pieces of writing that have the same topic and purpose but a different audience will often use very different language. This can be seen by the ways in which a children's comic and a dentists' leaflet both try to persuade people to eat sensibly.

SPECIAL WORDS
An important feature of using language well is to use the correct special names for things where suitable.

SWEET DREAMS
Two pieces of writing which provide information about the same topic but which are aimed at different audiences will often use very different language. They will also use different kinds of illustration.

MARIANNE DREAMS
The same factual material is treated very differently by the writer of a story, even though the story may contain quite a lot of straightforward information.

WANTED NEWS REPORTERS
There is a lot of skill in presenting information to an audience in the way that is right for them. The speaker or writer must know what the audience is expecting and be able to use words and sentences that fit in with this.

6 WORD PLAYS

WORD   PLAYS

WORD / PLAY

WORDS PLAY

WORD   PLAY

WORD   SPLAY

WORD   PLAY

SWORD PLAY

THE THINGS WE DO TO WORDS !

We use language for all sorts of important and useful things, but we also use it just for fun. In this chapter we look at some of the ways in which we play with words.

We use words to trick or puzzle people...   ...or to make them laugh...   We play games...   ...and we make up new words of our own.

WHAT'S THE DIFFERENCE BETWEEN A KANGAROO AND A BANANA ?

HAVE YOU HEARD THE JOKE ABOUT THE FROGMAN AND THE CARROT ?

WITH MY LITTLE EYE. SOMETHING BEGINNING WITH G.S.U

THERE WAS A YOUNG PERSON FROM CHATHAM.

How would you finish each of those ?

Old Mrs Thing-um-e-bob

Old Mrs Thing-um-e-bob,
  Lives at you-know-where.
Dropped her what-you-may-call it down
  The well of the kitchen stair.

'Gracious me !' said Thing-um-e-bob,
  'This don't look too bright.
I'll ask old Mr What's-his-name
  To try to put it right.'

Along came Mr What's-his-name,
  He said, 'You've broke the lot !
I'll have to see what I can do
  With some of the you-know-what.'

So he gave the what-you-may-call-it a pit
  And he gave it a bit of a pat,
And he put it all together again
  With a little of this and that.

And he gave the what-you-may-call-it a dib
  And he gave it a dab as well
When all of a sudden he heard a note
  As clear as any bell.

'It's as good as new !' cried What's-his-name
  'But please remember, now,
In future Mrs Thing-um-e-bob
  You'll have to go you-know-how.'

Charles Causley

So what happened ?

1 What are :

  a what-you-may-call-it

  the you-know-what

  a pit

  a bit of a pat

  a dib and a dab

2 How can Mrs Thing-um-e-bob go 'you-know-how' ?

3 Can you think of good names for the two people in the poem - names that really describe them ?

4 Where do you think 'you-know-where' is - what is a good place for someone like that to live ?

A story about Thingummy and What's-it

5 How many other words and phrases can you think of that people use instead of the proper names for things ? Make a list of them.

6 Now try using the words you have thought of - and the ones in the poem - in a piece of writing. It could be a story told by one person, or a conversation. Whichever you choose, use the words in your list so that it is not clear what is going on. (But - as in the poem - it must be possible to work it out with a bit of thought.)

Big trousers Dan

In the land of Rumplydoodle
where men eat jollips for tea,
and the cows in the hay
feel sleepy all day,
there's a wonderful sight to see.
On the banks of the River Bongbong,
in a hut made of turnips and cream,
sits a whiskery man,
name of Bigtrousers Dan,
and he plays with his brand new
machine.
There are gronfles
and nogglets
and pluffles
and valves that go
ker-pling and ker-plang,
and a big sugar wheel
that revolves with a squeal
till it's oiled with chocolate
meringue.
There are wurdlies
and flumdings
and crumchies
that go round as fast as they can,
and a big chocolate ball
that makes no sound at all
thanks to clever old
Bigtrousers Dan.

Peter Mortimer

WHAT KIND OF WORD ?
We can group words into classes, according to the ways in which they are used in sentences.

Nouns
All the nonsense words in the poem are nouns. We know this because of where they come in the sentences they are in:

> ...men eat *jollips* for tea...

You may not know what a jollip is, but you can think of plenty of things that will fit that space in the poem: **men eat -----s for tea** and they are all nouns. See how many words you can think of that will fit the space.

Singular and plural

Nouns follow rules. These rules will help you answer these questions:

If a man eats *jollips* for tea, does he eat one or more than one ? If it's more than one, what do we call just one ? If we talk about a number of *wurdlies* , what do we call (and how do we spell) just one ?

Adjectives
Make a list of all the words you can think of that will fit into the space in this sentence:

> **What I like best for tea is lots of ------ jollips.**

All the words you have chosen will help describe the jollips. As you probably know , they are called adjectives.

Verbs
See how many nonsense words you can make up that will fit this gap:

> Men ----- jollips all day.

Now make a list of five real words that will fit the same gap.

All the words you have listed are verbs - because only verbs will fit into that space in the sentence.

Nonsense dictionary
Make up a nonsense dictionary. Give definitions for all these words:

crumchy	flumding
gronfle	jollip
nogglet	pluffle
wurdlie	

PUNS JOKES & HOWLERS

In English there are many pairs of words that sound the same but have different meanings and spellings. There are also words which can have two (or more) very different meanings.

YES, HENRY IS A DEAR

SORT IT OUT

Each of these words has two different meanings (or more). What are they ?

light   bear   bow

train   pen

Say the words in the following list aloud. Can you think of another way of spelling the word you have said ? Write both words down and explain their meanings.

beach   place   bear

won   queue   I

CRAZY DEFINITIONS

Of course you can take puns a bit further and give words crazy meanings - especially if you pronounce them in the right way:

What crazy meanings can you give each of these words ?

tulips   kidney

goodbye   halo

lesson   each

Now think of some of your own.

aperitif

bison

robin

urchin

KNOCK KNOCK JOKES

These work in much the same way.

Knock knock	Knock knock
Who's there ?	Who's there ?
Arfer	Ewan
Arfer who ?	Ewan who ?
Arfer got.	Just me.

Try making up some knock knock jokes based on these names. The words in brackets are there to give you a clue about how you might use them.

Ida (I'd a...)

Gladys (Glad it's)

Harriet (Harry ate)

Les (Let's)

Watson

Olga

Michael

SHE WAS DRIVING A NEW WHITE HUNCHBACK

HOWLERS

Jokes are deliberate, but howlers are accidental - when we make a mistake because we confuse words or names.

I GAVE MY MUM A BUNCH OF LOVELY FRIESIANS

So what's wrong with each of these howlers ? What should they have said ?

1 A,E,I,O,and U are bowels.
2 Conservation is when you talk to people.
3 The Pope lives in the Vacuum.
4 A centimetre is an insect with 100 legs.
5 Philatelists were a race of people who lived in biblical times.
6 The Sewage Canal is in Egypt.

7 People who test your eyes to see if you need glasses are called optimists.
8 In France, everyone eats wine, even the pheasants.
9 Whales are hunted with large hairpins.
10 A hostage is a nice lady who serves drinks on aeroplanes.

An anagram is a word made up of the letters of another word. The best anagrams give us a clue to the meaning of the word they have been made from :

ENRAGED --> ANGERED

An anagram can also take the form of more than one word (a phrase):

WE STING --> TWINGES

WORK IT OUT

What is each of these words or phrases an anagram of ? (Some of them give you a clue; some of them don't.)

ANGER

HORSE

DIRER

IN GLASS

O FUN ! COINS !

A STEW SIR ?

VOICES RANT ON

CHEATING

A RAM SANG

Hint

It helps if you try grouping the letters in your word in patterns that are found in English words. For example in VOICES RANT ON, we find these common letter patterns: CON and TION. CON often comes at the beginning of words. TION is usually at the end. Can you think of any words that start with CON and end with TION ?

You try

Now try making up anagrams of your own, using this list of words:

MOPE

STOP

SLINK

POSTER

DENSER

RESIGN

ONE TO ANOTHER

Do you know how to turn hate into love ? It's easy:

HATE

DATE

DOTE

DOVE

LOVE

The rules of this word game are that you can only change one letter at a time and that you must always make a proper word.

Try these changes:

WET --> DRY

HOME --> AWAY

HEAD --> FOOT

word games

HEADS AND TAILS

The players choose a category, say animals. The first player then says the name of an animal, for example 'horse'. The second player then has to think of an animal that begins with the last letter of 'horse', **e** : elephant, and so on:

Charlie:	Horse
Di:	Elephant
Eric:	Tiger
Freda:	Rabbit

You must not repeat a word or name that has already been said. When someone can't think of an animal, they are out and the others choose a new category. To start you off, here are some categories:

Birds

Plants and flowers

Towns

Countries

First names

Titles of books or TV programmes

The last person left in is the winner.

ACROSTICS

The players begin by choosing a word. To start off with it's best to choose a word of five to seven letters that doesn't contain any 'awkward customers' like X or Z. Everybody writes it down like this:

B

R

E

A

D

Then you choose a category, such as 'flowers and plants'. Each player then has to think of one kind of flower or plant that begins with each of the letters:

Buttercup

R

Eidelweiss

A

D

You can score in various ways. One is that you count one point for every letter in every word you have written down.

GHOSTS

This is a kind of spelling game. The first player says a letter. The second player adds another letter that could begin to build up a word:

Georgina:	D
Harry:	R

The next player then adds a third that will help to build up a word, but she must not finish a word. If she does, she is out. So if Irma says 'Y', she's out because she has completed the word 'DRY'.

Irma:	E (She is thinking of 'Dream')
John:	N (He is thinking of 'Drench')

If one of the other players thinks that the letter that has been added will not go towards a real word, they can challenge it. Then the person who said the letter has to defend it by saying the word they were thinking of:

Kate:	C
Leo:	Challenge. There's no such word.
Kate:	Yes there is - 'Drench''.

And Leo is out. If the challenge is successful, then the person who said the letter is out. The game goes on until there is only one person left.

word plays sell

Puns and jokes and other games with words are often used in advertisements.

Thanks to £1,100 Gas Central Heating I'm down to my bare-skin!

ATTENTION! Eyes right...and you'll meet Kensington Ken. He's one Private who just loves to go public.

It's all due to £1,100 Gas Central Heating, of course. Says Ken, 'I felt at ease with the price, because I didn't even need to rifle my savings.

'I quick-marched to my local Gas Showroom. They were round...at the double...armed with five radiators and a boiler!

'No more soldiering on with the cold for me...now I'm a HOT SHOT!!'

Put your life in your hands

...with the new Canon ...to grasp.

...e grip, with all ...o that high or ...th function ... but can ...keep your ...from the

...zones ...perfect

The E640 is packed with useful features: Canon 8 x zoom; Hi-Fi Sound; Digital Titler; Self Timer and Interval Timer; 4 Mode High Speed Shutter; fade in/out and high speed search are just a few.

Just get the feel of the E640 and you won't want to put it down, except to watch the results, with the help of a multi-function remote control.

Canon E640
VIDEO CAMERA

More clean socks. Less square feet.

Persil automatic

40 cm

A cinema attendant has been letting a queue of people into the cinema but the cinema is full. The attendant puts up the 'House Full' sign just as two boys reach the front of the queue. One of the boys is holding a packet of Golden Wonder Wotsits. The attendant stops them going in

Attendant :	That's it.
Boys :	What's it ?
Attendant :	*(Taking a Wotsit from the packet)* Oh thanks.
	Look, it's horrible anyway.
1st Boy :	My brother's seen it.
Attendant :	It'll give you the what's-it's.
2nd Boy :	We've already got the Wotsits.
Attendant :	You look all right to me.

The boys groan

Attendant :	All right - what's it worth ?

Attendant grabs the bag of Wotsits and starts eating them. He smiles a sickly smile.

Cheesers - delightfully cheesy - just melt in the mouth.

The attendant turns away and starts walking towards the cinema entrance, still holding the bag of Wotsits. He trips over and falls flat on his face. He leaves go of the Wotsits and they land in one of the boys' hands.The boys grin at each other and run into the cinema. The attendant slowly straightens up and then realises what has happened.

Attendant :	What's it to me ?

How do they work ?

Adverts like these only work for people who speak the language very well. Imagine how difficult they would be to understand if you were just starting to learn English. For each of the adverts:

1 Say which of the words are being used in a funny (or punny) way.

2 Explain what the word(s) usually mean.

3 Explain what they mean here - and how the joke or play on words works.

Now you try

See if you can make up a jokey advertisement. You can invent one of these:

- a jingle (advertising song or rhyme)

- a slogan or catch phrase

- a full magazine advert

- a full TV or radio advert

And you can advertise one of these...

Porky links (small sausages)

'Smine (sweets you don't want to share)

Gulp (a new fizzy drink)

...or make up a product of your own.

What do you make of this?

What are the missing words?

RIDDLES

Riddles are puzzles or tricks with words. When you know the answer, they're obvious. When you don't they can be infuriating. Some riddles work by simple tricks:

A man who lives near us has a big pear tree. It has 22 main branches and each of these has 8 branches coming off it. Each of these has 6 boughs coming off it and each bough leads to 9 twigs. On each twig there is a fruit. How many apples are there on the tree?

Some riddles work by giving a strange explanation or definition of something:

> Has eighty-eight keys
>   And needs no more,
> But can't unlock
>   A single door.

> 'Tis true I have both face and hands,
>   And move before your eyes;
> Yet when I go my body stands
>   And when I stand I lie.

And some of course, are just infuriating:

Other riddles play on words, as puns and 'Knock knock' jokes do:

> Take away my first letter; take away my second letter; take away my third letter; all right take away all my letters, and yet I remain the same. What am I ?

> Why is an empty room like a room full of married people ?

WHAT'S GREEN WITH PURPLE SPOTS, HAS A LONG TRUNK AND BURROWS THROUGH THE GROUND AT A HUNDRED MILES PER HOUR ?

I DUNNO ... WHAT IS ?

NOTHING

OLD ENGLISH RIDDLES

Hundreds of years ago, riddles were very popular with the ancestors of the English, the Anglo-Saxons. Their riddles were often made up by poets, who enjoyed describing things in strange and puzzling ways.

> On the way a miracle: water become bone.

> On earth there's a warrior of curious origin.
> He's created, gleaming, by two dumb creatures
> For the benefit of men. Foe bears him against foe
> To inflict harm. Women often fetter him,
> Strong as he is. If maidens and men
> Care for him with due consideration
> And feed him frequently, he'll faithfully obey them
> And serve them well. Men succour him for the warmth
> He offers in return; but this warrior will cruelly punish
> Anyone who permits him to become too proud.

follow-up

PUN BANK

Try using words from this list of puns to make up your own riddles, jokes or adverts.

be/bee	beat/beet	board/bored	caught/court
eye/I	find/fined	grease/Greece	great/grate
might/might/mite	port	rain/reign	real/reel
sure/shore	team/teem	through/threw	toe/tow
wails/Wales			

summary

We enjoy playing with words as well as using them seriously in our daily lives.

OLD MRS THING-UM-E-BOB

We get pleasure from nonsense poems, but they also illustrate how our language works. Even when the words in a poem are made up they still follow the same grammatical rules as real words.

PUNS JOKES AND HOWLERS

Some words in English have two or more very different meanings. There are also pairs of words that sound the same but are spelled differently and have different meanings. The same can apply to phrases. These similarities are the basis of puns, jokes (including 'Knock, knock' jokes) and howlers.

ANAGRAMS

Some word games, such as anagrams and 'One to another' help us to see that spelling follows certain patterns (or 'rules') and that we often understand these patterns better than we realise.

WORD GAMES

Other word games like 'Heads and tails', 'Acrostics', and 'Ghosts' are fun to play, but also give us practice in spelling.

WORDPLAYS SELL

These forms of word play are often used by advertisers to make their products attractive by bringing them to our attention in an entertaining way.

Useful words

accent (p52)

The way in which words and sentences are pronounced in a particular area, or by a particular group of speakers.

acrostic (p87)

A poem or other piece of writing in which the first, middle or last letter of each line form a word, name or saying.

acrostic
Mighty winds roar
As this month begins,
Ruining trees, and
Checking our growing
Hopes for the spring.

adjective (p83)

A class of words that work with nouns. Adjectives qualify nouns: they make their meaning clearer or fuller.

adverb

A class of words that work with verbs, adjectives or other adverbs. They modify these words: they make their meaning clearer or fuller.

adjectives
I've lost my book. It's a **large, blue, hardback** dictionary.

anagram (p86)

A rearrangement of the letters of a word or phrase to make another word or phrase.

borrowing (p20)

A word which comes into one language from another. (Or the process by which this happens.)

adverbs
She was running **quickly**.
She's a **really very** fast runner.

brand name (16)

The name given to a particular product by the manufacturer, or the manufacturer's name when it is applied to the product. Such words sometimes come into the language and are used as ordinary nouns (eg Thermos, Hoover.)

derivation
The word **canyon** derives from the Spanish word *cañon*, meaning a pipe. This in turn comes from the Spanish *cana*, or 'cane'.

consonant (p37)

(1) The letters bcdfghjklmnpqrstvwxyz.
(2) Speech sounds which are made by blocking the mouth and or throat in some way.

derivation

Where a word derives, or comes from.

dialect (p54) — The form of language used in a particular area or by a particular group. A dialect may contain words that are not used elsewhere and may also include special grammatical forms.

dictionary (p26) — A word book arranged in alphabetical order, giving meanings and other information about words.

etymology — (1) The study of where words come from. (2) The description of the derivation of a particular word.

howler (p84) — Mistaking one word for another that is similar and thus causing amusement without meaning to.

idiom (p15) — A popular expression used by native speakers of a language. Idioms are often difficult for foreigners to understand because they use words in unexpected ways.

lexicographer (p28) — A person who writes, or helps to write, a dictionary.

loan word — A word which comes from another language. (see 'borrowing'.)

mother tongue — The language that a person learns first (from their mother).

native speaker — Someone who speaks a language as their mother tongue.

nonsense verse (p82) — Poems in which the meaning is deliberately crazy or absurd.

---

etymology

The etymology of the word **dandelion** is interesting, because it shows how our language developed. In the middle ages, the plant was called, in Latin, *dens leonis*, or lion's tooth. This referred to the jagged edge of the leaves. The name was then translated into French : *dent-de-lion*, which was gradually changed into the name we know today.

howlers

In the Old Testament, Jacob's brother was called see-saw.

Egypt is famous for the Sewage Canal.

An autobiography is the life story of a motor car.

idioms

Some English idioms that foreigners find difficult:

You scratch my back and I'll scratch yours.

The house was all shipshape and Bristol fashion.

This is a pretty kettle of fish and no mistake.

loan words

café (French)

spaghetti (Italian)

thug (Hindi)

noun (p83)	a class of words referring to people, places, things and ideas.
onomatopoeia (p41)	Forming or using words that imitate sounds.
part of speech (p26)	See 'word class'.
phrase	A group of words that forms part of a sentence. A phrase makes some sense, but not the full sense that a sentence does.
pronunciation (p26)	How words are spoken.
pun (p84)	A play on words, using either (a) a word that has two distinct meanings (like 'light') or (b) two words that sound the same but are written differently (like 'weight' and 'wait'.)
Received pronunciation (p52)	An accent used throughout Britain by a large group of educated and influential speakers of English. (Often shortened to 'RP'.)
rhythm (p40)	Poetry often has a more-or-less regular pattern of strong and weak beats in each line. This is its rhythm.
riddle (p90)	A puzzle in words.
RP (p52)	See 'Received Pronunciation'.
sentence	A group of words that makes complete sense and is grammatically complete.

nouns

My **brother John** went to the **station** in **Birmingham** and caught a **train** to **London**, but it was all a **mistake**.

onomatopoeia

Some onomatopoeic words:

rumble, twitter, splash, clatter.

phrase and **sentence**

These are **sentences**:

I love large peppermint chocolate ice-creams.

I should have been going to the fair today.

He threw the ball right out of the playground.

These are **phrases**:

large peppermint chocolate ice-creams

should have been going

right out of the playground

slang (p32)

A form of language that is not standard. It often contains words or phrases that are only understood by (and suitable for) a particular group of people (eg school slang.)

slang and **Standard English**

slang : 'D'you want a punch up the bracket ?'

Standard English : 'Would you like a punch on the nose ?'

Standard English (p52)

A form of English which is understood throughout England. It is normally used for writing and for speech in formal situations.

synonym (p30)

A word having the same meaning as (or very similar meaning to) another word.

technical term

A word or phrase with a specialist meaning.

synonym

Synonyms for **happy**: contented joyful cheerful

thesaurus (p30)

A word book that groups together words of a similar meaning.

transcribe (p44)

To write down the actual words someone speaks. A written version of this kind is called a 'transcript'.

verb (p26)

A class of words that refer to actions or states. A sentence normally contains a verb.

verbs

I **should like to go** to Edinburgh this year, especially since I **have** never **visited** Scotland.

vowel (p37)

(1) The letters a e i o u.

(2) Speech sounds that are made with the mouth and throat open and unblocked.

word class (p26)

Words can be grouped according to the ways in which they are used in a sentence. These groups (such as 'nouns' and 'verbs') are called 'word classes'. They are also sometimes called 'parts of speech'.